Traveling
the **Path** of
Compassion

Traveling the Path of Compassion

His Holiness the Gyalwang Karmapa

A Commentary on
The Thirty-Seven Practices of a Bodhisattva
by Ngülchu Thogme

Oral translation by Ringu Tulku and Michele Martin
Translation of the Root Text and editing by Michele Martin

Volume 19   Number 2
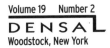
Woodstock, New York

KTD Publications

Published by *Densal* and KTD Publications
335 Meads Mountain Road
Woodstock, New York 12498
© 2009 by Karma Triyana Dharmachakra
Root verses © 1992, 1994, 2000, 2009 by Michele Martin

Cover and interior design by Naomi Schmidt
Cover photo by Sarite Sanders, 2008
Back cover photo by Robert Hanson-Storm, 2008
Distribution by Namse Bangdzo Bookstore
335 Meads Mountain Road
Woodstock, New York 12498
www.NamseBangdzo.com

Printed in the USA on recycled acid-free paper.

ISBN 978-1-934608-06-7

Contents

Preface

THE *THIRTY-SEVEN PRACTICES OF A BODHISATTVA* is one of the most beloved texts in Tibet. Rich in imagery, it distills the essentials for practice into a few pages and gives them into our hands. Its author, Ngülchu Thogme Zangpo, was a great scholar and a practitioner of the utmost simplicity. This blend of depth and openness is continued in the commentary by His Holiness the Seventeenth Karmapa. His language is not academic and yet the topics discussed cover the perennial questions of scholars and practitioners alike. With the fresh glance of his youth, he is able to find the key point of each verse and make it relevant to where we are today. The Karmapa also draws on personal experience, reaching out to the reader with stories from his own life to illuminate many of the points he is making.

The Karmapa further resembles Thogme Zangpo in following a literary tradition of profound humility, common in Tibetan texts. It even has a name, *kheng pa pong wa*, which means "discarding arrogance." In the closing verses, for example,

Thogme Zangpo apologizes for his poor composition that will hardly appeal to scholars, and in the Karmapa's commentary, he makes disclaimers that he knows little, has limited experience, and so forth. Needless to say, these are not to be taken literally. Another aspect of his style is that the Karmapa does not announce his sense of humor, which can be subtle.

The teachings that comprise *Traveling the Path of Compassion* were given at Tilokpur Nunnery in northern India during February 2007, right after the Tibetan New Year, which is considered a very auspicious time. Originally, they were to be made available through *Densal*, a semiannual publication, which features the teachings of the Karmapa and other lamas who visit Karma Triyana Dharmachakra, his main seat in the United States. Upon reflection, however, it seemed best to present this series of talks all together and the Karmapa agreed, so *Densal* Vol. 19 No. 2 has become *Traveling the Path of Compassion*. In the spring of 2008, the Karmapa gave additional commentary to round out his presentation for the book, and this was incorporated during the editing process.

The Thirty-Seven Practices of a Bodhisattva is the first full-length text with the Karmapa's commentary to appear in translation. As he is an emanation of Chenrezik, the bodhisattva of compassion, it is fitting that the Karmapa began with this revered text, for it invokes Chenrezik at the beginning and end, and in the middle teaches how to develop our compassion and wisdom so that we may become bodhisattvas as well.

May the Karmapa's life be long and his activity flourish.
May all living beings move swiftly along the path
   to full awakening.

CHAPTER 1

Preparing the Ground

W HATEVER IT IS I KNOW, I will do my best to pass along to you, and if you receive it joyfully, then our minds will make a connection. What I really have to transmit to you is the blessing of the lineage, and since I am a follower of the Kagyü lineage, it will be the blessing of this tradition. It is not only words that you should receive but a blessing along with precise oral instructions that can have a deep effect. With my limited ability, I will do the best I can. What comes to mind I will say, and through the translators, my speech will come to you. Since you are sensitive and show a lively interest, it could be beneficial.

The Dharma is not something that affects us immediately. When we are hungry, we eat and are satisfied right away. Nor does it take that long to build a house. But it is difficult to feel an immediate benefit right after learning about Dharma, because the Dharma depends on a process, and we must become familiar with it. As our mind is turned toward Dharma, our way of thinking will shift over time. When our thinking changes, so will our life. It is possible that our life may become both good for ourselves and useful to others.

In the world today, technology is developing at a very fast pace. If we look into its nature, we will find that technology is a neutral phenomenon: it can bring benefit and it can bring harm. Whether it turns into one or the other does not depend on the technology but on the people who make or use it. What are their motivations? How will they use what they have created? When we say that the use of technology depends on people, it means that whether someone is young or old, famous or unknown, with a wish to help others, whatever they do will bring benefit.

In olden times, certain people protected the peace and security while others fought for freedom or protected human rights; all of them were regarded as heroes. It was as if some people were special, but it is not like that now. In our age of worldwide communication, everyone has responsibility and everyone can become a hero who defends peace, freedom, and well-being. If the question is "Who is the hero?" the answer is "He is, she is, you are—everyone is."

These days progress is being made through material, industrial, and technical advances, which are very good. There is nothing wrong with them. We could not stop them even if we wanted to, and it would be wrong to try. We have to make progress. But along with it, we need to take responsibility, because problems accompany progress, and we need to face them. If we are not prepared to do that, progress will run away from us. The inevitable problems will arise, but we will not pay attention to them and lose the mind-set that knows the importance of taking action. There is a great danger that the world could be approaching destruction. Whether this actually happens or not depends on all of us, not just a few. No matter who we are, if we have a positive motivation and discernment, we can take this responsibility of seeing that our good intentions are realized. We may live in a remote corner of the world, but what we are doing is for the whole world. In our heart we feel love and compassion for all sentient beings and intend to do something that will be beneficial for them.

In the beginning, we purify ourselves in the same way that gold is refined. When a piece of gold ore is first taken from the ground, it does not look like a precious metal, because it is mixed together with impurities. When these are removed, the essence of the ore, pure gold, appears. In the same way, within our mind there is much that is beneficial and much that is harmful as well. Our work is to clear away the impure and harmful and take up the pure and beneficial. Then, when this pure gold of our mind is revealed, we will really be able to help the world.

CHAPTER 2

A Few Words on Buddhism

OVER THE LAST THREE THOUSAND YEARS, many different spiritual traditions have appeared, and they can be divided into two types. One type has established tenets, a system of philosophy, while the other does not have a clearly developed philosophical system but does have a strong structure of belief. This can involve, for example, worshipping something in the natural world like the sun or the moon.

Buddhism is a religion with clear philosophical tenets, based on examination and investigation, and established through reasoning. Within Buddhism, we have two broad schools. One of these depends mostly on devotion to the Buddha or placing confidence in his teachings and scriptures, while the other school places greater emphasis on reasoning and analysis. Tibetan Buddhism is part of this second system. It has four lineages, which are based on a gradual path of investigation and not just on following the teachings as they are inherited. The step-by-step process taught by these four lineages is based on a profound examination that looks from many different angles in order to discover the way things really are.

The Thirty-Seven Practices of a Bodhisattva belongs to the Mahayana (the Great Vehicle) tradition and is based on the Madhyamaka (the Middle Way) school of philosophy, which advocates the use of analysis to attain clear understanding and omniscient wisdom. It also encourages the practice of the six paramitas, or perfections: generosity, discipline, patience, diligence, meditative concentration, and deeper knowing or superior intelligence. So that the first five of these perfections come into their own, they must be embraced by the sixth, deeper knowing. The teachings contained in *The Thirty-Seven Practices* are based on the teachings of the Buddha and also on teachings and commentaries given by the great masters of India.

The Buddha's teachings (Kangyur in Tibetan) can be divided in many ways. One way is to divide them into three collections of scripture known as the Tripitaka—the vinaya (monastic discipline), sutra (discourses), and abhidharma (higher knowledge or phenomenology). Or they could be thought of as the four levels of tantra, and so forth. The Tibetan collection of commentaries on the Buddha's teachings is called the Tengyur. Although translations into Tibetan started very early, even now we find that many teachings of the Buddha have not yet been translated. Buddhist scriptures and the authoritative texts of the great masters in India were mainly written in Sanskrit or Pali. Later, countless commentaries and important works were written by many great masters in China, Tibet, and other countries.

Within Buddhism, there are three principal paths or vehicles—the Theravada (the Way of the Elders), the Mahayana (the Great Vehicle), and the Vajrayana (the Vajra or Adamantine Vehicle). Even in ancient India, many disputes and discussions arose about the differences among these paths. For instance, there were debates about whether the Mahayana teachings were actually taught by the Buddha. Much of the early literature sought to establish that the Mahayana teachings did indeed originate in the Buddha's own words. These statements were supported by citing scripture as well as establishing its view through reasoning. Likewise, there have been doubts about whether the Vajrayana teachings belong to what the Buddha himself taught.

These doubts are not without reason. For example, there are words in the Vajrayana teachings that do not mean exactly what they seem to mean, but express something beyond their usual connotations. Some aspects of the Vajrayana are profound and complex and are not meant for everyone. For this reason, people have recommended that such teachings be kept secret from those who are not suited for the practice. It is important to understand that different types of people are able to receive different levels of teachings. When people are attracted to Buddhist teachings, they should determine which ones are appropriate for them. It is not necessary for every Buddhist practitioner to completely understand all three levels of teachings. However, when actually studying and meditating on the Vajrayana, we should understand its true meaning and deeper significance. In Tibet, we study and practice within this tradition of the Vajrayana.

In the past, many great masters practiced at the two great Buddhist universities in India, Nalanda and Vikramashila. These masters were very learned and highly realized, and they promulgated the genuine teachings of the Vajrayana by composing practices and giving oral instructions. For instance, Nagarjuna, the founder of Madhyamaka philosophy, wrote numerous practices, commentaries, and special instructions on a variety of tantras and Vajrayana teachings. His students Aryadeva and Chandrakirti followed his example, composing both analytical and tantric texts. Like other scholars at Nalanda, the great master Naropa also practiced and taught the Vajrayana. In sum, when we look into history, we find that those masters who practiced and taught the Vajrayana were, beyond any dispute, considered Buddhist.

This history of scholarship shows that Buddhism is not just a belief system based on faith. In practicing the Dharma, we develop wisdom through using our intelligence and the power of reasoning. By listening, reflecting, and meditating, we clear away doubts and develop our ability to analyze with reasonings. First, we listen and study in order to learn the various presentations of the Dharma. Then, through reflecting we turn questions over in our mind and use many types of reasoning to develop certainty. Finally, through meditation we blend our mind together with the certainty in the view that we have established.

When we decide to practice bodhichitta—the intention to attain awakening for the sake of all living beings—we are not just trying to understand the meaning of the word. Studying and reflecting are not enough. Whether it is love and compassion, or whether it is bodhichitta, just to say, "Love means this" and "Bodhichitta means that" is not enough. We have to experience what bodhichitta means so clearly and so strongly that it becomes one with our mind and blends with our way of being. If that does not happen, we will only have a conceptual understanding rather than something we have experienced ourselves.

When we study and reflect on a teaching, we should choose a text that provides a broad understanding of the Buddha's teaching as a whole. The great master Atisha said that within all the sciences there is so much to know that one lifetime would not suffice. We do not have the time to study every one of the teachings of the Buddha, and life is too short to go through every commentary or root text. Therefore, we choose a text that allows us to know everything by studying a single one; like the rising sun, it can illuminate all things. A famous statement runs: Knowing one, you know all. Studying a particular text in depth, we can cut through all doubts, so there is a great benefit to narrowing our focus in this way.

The Thirty-Seven Practices of a Bodhisattva is this kind of text. It is mainly a teaching on mind training from the Kadampa tradition. In Tibet, many great masters from all the lineages have studied, reflected, and meditated on this text, and they have also written commentaries and taught it. The Thirty-Seven Practices of a Bodhisattva is considered both deep and broad, comprehensive and concise. It includes all of the necessary points for understanding the practices of a bodhisattva.

Before we begin with the the actual text, however, it is important to know something about the author, Ngülchu Thogme Zangpo. If we do not say something about him, it might seem as if his teaching just fell from the sky. It will help to make a connection with his words if we know that they were written by someone who is made of flesh and bones like us and also experienced both happiness and suffering.

CHAPTER 3

Portrait of Thogme Zangpo

GÜLCHU THOGME ZANGPO (1295–1369) was born in the U-Tsang region of Tibet near Shakya Monastery. When he was very young, his name was Konchok Zangpo. We know that great individuals come out of great hardships, and this is also true for Thogme Zangpo. From very early childhood, he faced a great many difficulties. His mother passed away when he was three. Afterward his grandmother looked after him, but she passed away in the same year. Finally, an uncle taught and cared for him, providing Thogme Zangpo with all he needed when he became a monk at the age of fourteen. When he was twenty-nine, Thogme Zangpo took the full ordination of a bhikshu.

During his early study of Dharma, Thogme Zangpo was taught by many Sakya scholars, who covered Madhyamaka and Chittamatra (Mind-Only) teachings, as well as the different kinds of bodhichitta vows. He also received numerous empowerments, reading transmissions, key instructions, and commentaries from these Sakya masters. Further, he heard and practiced many Dzogchen (Great Perfection) instructions. Thereafter, he received teachings from all of the other lineages and schools, practicing them all impartially.

When he was fifteen years old, the other monks gave him a new name. They called him Thogme, which in Tibetan means "that which cannot be blocked by any obstacles" or "unstoppable. He received this name when he was studying in a monastery that had established a seminary and a debating courtyard. A great scholar, Nyima Gyaltsen, had come to teach *The Compendium of Knowledge (Abhidharmakosha)*, a fundamental text by the well-known Indian master Asanga. The scholar held a debate on the abhidharma and introduced the concept of experiencing suffering without afflictions. He asked his students, "Freedom from afflictions and suffering are contradictory. What is the common basis they both share? How is it that they are not in contradiction?" In other words, how is it possible to have suffering without afflictions, since when afflictions are absent there is no cause for suffering?

At first no one could reply. Then Thogme, who was only fifteen years old at the time, came up with the answer. He said, "Some arhants (realized masters) from the traditions of the Hearers and Solitary Sages still experience suffering through the impelling force of their karma." And this was the right answer, for arhants have overcome their afflictions, but some still suffer due to their karma. Thogme Zangpo had found an example that gave a common basis for two seemingly contradictory statements. Everyone was so impressed with this answer that they called him Thogme, the Tibetan for Asanga. Everyone present, both other scholars and his own teachers, said, "You are really like the great master Asanga."

Not only did Thogme Zangpo become an accomplished scholar, he also became a great practitioner. Having realized the equality between self and other, he knew how to exchange himself with others. When Thogme Zangpo was about thirty years old, a beggar who was infested with lice appeared at the gate of his monastery. Thogme Zangpo understood that if people knew such a person were staying near the gate, they would probably drive him away. So Thogme secretly brought food and supplies to the beggar under cover of darkness. This went on for a few days, but then one night Thogme Zangpo did not find the man, so he searched all over for him. Finally, he discovered the wretched beggar hiding in a corner.

He asked him, "Why are you doing this? Why didn't I see you before?"

The beggar replied, "I'm hiding because anyone who sees me is so repulsed by my appearance, they feel nauseous. So I try to stay out of their way."

The man looked so miserable that Thogme Zangpo took him to his own room and let him stay there. He brought him more food and gave him one of his own robes, a nice woolen garment, to replace the rags infested by lice. Then it occurred to Thogme Zangpo that if these old clothes were thrown away, all the lice would die, since they live off blood. To keep that from happening, he took the beggar's clothes and put them on himself.

From wearing this infested clothing, he became really sick, so sick that he could not give teachings anymore. His students came to find out what was happening, and when they saw what was going on, they all protested. Some said, "To be a Dharma practitioner, you don't need to get involved in other people's sufferings and troubles. You can practice Dharma and also lead a comfortable life." Other people said, "You are wasting your time. It is not good to ruin your precious life for something as insignificant as lice." Other students simply requested, "For the sake of your students, please don't do this. Please get rid of the lice and put on some fresh clothes."

Thogme Zangpo smiled and answered them, "So far I have had many lives, and all of them went to waste because I focused on myself. This time I am using my body and my life to help others. Now I have a purpose and feel useful. Even if I die now, I will know that I used my years in a meaningful way. So I'm not going to change what I'm doing. I will not give this up."

He continued wearing the beggar's clothes for some seventeen days, nurturing the lice until all of them were gone. It seems that they died from overeating. In any case, after they had all passed away, Thogme Zangpo gathered them up and, as one would for humans, made tsa-tsa (small sacred images) out of them. Then with prayers and mantras, he conducted a kind of last rites for the departed lice.

That was a story about exchanging our comfort for the suffering of others. Here is another story about how Thogme Zangpo incorporated difficult situations into his life and onto the path.

Once when he was very ill, one of his students asked, "What kind of illness do you have?"

Thogme replied, "This is a very special illness."

"What can we do to get rid of this illness?"

"There is nothing to get rid of," said the teacher. "I just pray to the Triple Gem, saying to the Buddha, Dharma, and Sangha that if my being sick is good for other beings, bless me with sickness. If it is good that I die, bless me with death. If it is good that I get well, bless me with health. I make these prayers, but I don't do anything to get rid of the illness." Like this, Thogme Zangpo used his illness joyfully as a way of practicing along the path. With these examples, we can see that Thogme Zangpo did not just create the words of this text; he actually put them into practice.

When he was on his deathbed, friends and students came to see him, knowing that these were his last days. One of his students asked, "After you die, in which pure land will you take birth?"

Thogme Zangpo replied, "There are some Kadampa masters who pray to be reborn in the hell realm, and I too would be happy to be born there if it would be useful to living beings. If my rebirth were not beneficial to others, it would not be good for me, even if I were reborn in a pure land. I have no desire for such a rebirth. Anyway, I don't have the power to be reborn wherever I wish. I just pray that I will be reborn in a place where I will be able to help sentient beings."

One of his best students, Panglo Chenpo, used to say to his own students, "If you want to become like me, you'll have to accumulate positive deeds for a just few lifetimes. But if you want to become like my teacher, Thogme Zangpo, you'll have to accumulate positive deeds for a great number of lifetimes."

So that is the story of Ngülchu Thogme Zangpo, who wrote *The Thirty-Seven Practices of a Bodhisattva*. We may have found that some of this account made us a little bit uncomfortable, especially the part about having to go through numerous lifetimes. But Thogme Zangpo was a very great master and bodhisattva, who dedicated his life to helping all living beings and accomplishing a vast ocean of merit. Anyone who aspires to his state of being will probably have to accumulate many positive deeds for numerous lifetimes.

When we talk about lifetimes, we usually mean that we have to be born, go through life, and die over and over again. In another sense, however, it may be possible that many lifetimes' accumulation of positive deeds can occur in a few moments. It is all about skillful means. If we can accumulate positive deeds in a powerful way—if we have wisdom and compassion and our actions are done in a proper way on the right spot—then it is not impossible to accumulate the good work of many lifetimes, even many eons. An eon's accumulation of merit can happen in a very short time.

All of the great masters of the past and all of the bodhisattvas have aspired to benefit every living being. In the same way, each one of us can make this aspiration. I pray that all of us, just like Thogme Zangpo, will be able to accomplish a great benefit for all living beings.

CHAPTER 4
How to
View Emptiness

I N MADHYAMAKA TEXTS, teachings about emptiness, or no self, are given very clearly with abundant reasonings and quotes from scripture. However, these teachings are so profound and vast that even teachers who belong to the same system of Madhyamaka philosophy approach them in different ways; for example, there are many ways to explain the nature of mind. Despite all this diversity, what cannot be overturned or abandoned is the fundamental position asserted by the Madhyamaka: the unity of emptiness and dependent arising. The two arise together and are inseparable. Emptiness does not conflict with dependent arising, and likewise, dependent arising does not conflict with emptiness. This profound unity of emptiness and dependent arising is the ultimate view of all those who understand Buddhist philosophy in depth.

The first line of the homage, "Seeing that all phenomena neither come nor go," refers to freedom from all mental elaborations or constructs. What do we mean by this term *mental construct*? It refers to the myriad ways our minds grasp on to objects or phenomena. For example, a mental construct can refer to a concept that takes something to exist or not exist. It can refer to a concept that assumes something to be true or not, or a concept that takes something to belong to samsara or nirvana, or that views an event in terms of something coming or going. All these ways of grasping are often summarized into eight types: arising and cessation, extinction and permanence, coming and going, separate and the same. One of these pairs, "coming and going," is found in the first line of the verse. Since the true nature of phenomena is beyond all mental constructs, the verse states that an enlightened being such as Chenrezik sees that "all phenomena neither come nor go." Ultimately, therefore, every mental construct is empty of true existence.

There is much to be said about another pair of mental constructs, existence and nonexistence, which are fundamental concepts in Buddhist philosophy. One approach is to view them from different perspectives. The first perspective can be framed as the statement "A phenomenon that merely exists is empty." This level of "mere existence" relates to dependent arising or conventional reality. Without this, there would be nothing appearing to ordinary individuals. Therefore we avoid saying that things do not "exist," but instead say that they are "merely existent." A second perspective can be framed in the statement "Phenomena truly exist." It is this second perspective, which takes things to be truly existent, that we want to negate, because it forms the basis of ego-fixation, obscurations, and suffering. Understanding what we need to reject allows us to see clearly that the way our mind takes things to be real is based on an illusion, or in other words, phenomena do not exist in the way we think they do.

The emptiness of phenomena is explained in many commentaries and from different points of view. But for an ordinary individual, whose intellect is untrained and therefore rather coarse, it can be difficult to analyze appearances and thus discover their empty nature. Why so? Because from long habituation our mind invariably wants to grasp on to phenomena (for example, the "I" that we so cherish) as being truly existent. This is one reason study is so important. It allows us to analyze phenomena and come to understand their true nature: or how they exist (merely) and do not exist (truly or ultimately).

Two Ways of Approaching View

We have to discover for ourselves a deeper way of seeing, and we do so by searching. There are two ways to find this deeper way: we can approach it from the positive side or we can come from the negative side. The first line of the verse, "Seeing that all phenomena neither come nor go," uses negation to go beyond mental constructs. Most of the major texts use this process of elimination to arrive at a conclusion or an understanding. Another way of approaching view is to come from the positive side, which is a perspective mostly found in oral instructions and practice manuals. This method makes use of affirmative statements, such as "You do this or that, and you will experience such and such." or "Do not do this. Give it up." In this way we are guided directly, not through negation but in a positive, more experiential way. In the beginning, however, it is better for practitioners to start with negation since there is little harm and great benefit.

When we talk about trying to find the truth from the positive side, we can imitate the scientists whose research is based on exterior objects. We do not try to analyze phenomena using reason alone, looking to see whether a phenomenon is existent or nonexistent. Instead, we go directly to an object such as a pillar or a vase and examine it to see whether it exists or not. When scientists investigate the subtle structure of a particle, they do not think about what appears in their minds, but go directly to the object and examine it from many different directions. The facts that scientists establish through their investigations allow them to discover the characteristic nature of the object they are exploring. As a result of this process, they become certain about what it is.

Following their example, we can find a much clearer view, and be more confident in what we discover, by paying careful attention to the object itself. This helps us to realize that it is not just something in our subjective mind. This is important because when we are thinking subjectively, we are actually focused on the concepts arising in our mind. If we think objectively, however, and focus on an aspect of the object *as it appears*, it can remain stable and clear. It is very important, I think, to try to look at phenomena objectively and to observe the object of the investigation itself more directly. If we can do this without looking to see if the object is real or not and, further, if we are working with the profound oral instructions of a lama and maintaining an unwavering mind, then through working with the view, we really will be able to find the definitive meaning, or ultimate reality. So there are two approaches, negation and assertion, and we need both, for they complement each other.

"I" and "Mine" on Center Stage

When seeking out a view or philosophical position, some people look for one that is easy to comprehend and not complicated to explain. This is the one they hold up as the best. But, really, all they have found is a view that fits their way of thinking. To discover a view that transcends the world of our mundane thought is actually quite difficult. We are always looking for what we want to find. For example, if we are enamored of gold, we will look everywhere for places that sell gold and purchase the best we can find. If we are very fond of flowers, we will not look for jewelers or gold merchants, but seek out florists and buy from them. Wanting gold, we fixate on gold; wanting flowers, we fixate on flowers. We are following the trail of our concepts, unable to go beyond them.

What happens then? Tracking our wants, we develop a stupendous clinging to ourselves ("I") and what we think is ours ("mine"). This fixation on ourselves comes along without any basis or foundation whatsoever. This happens because through the power of our habitual patterns even though thinking in terms of "I" and "mine" does not meet any valid logical criteria these concepts seem to be well founded. This comes about because, from time beyond time, we have been taking phenomena to be truly existent. This way of thinking may not be obvious to us, but it is in fact deeply embedded in our habitual patterns. This is why it seems natural that "I" and "mine" seem real, and why we take these concepts to be positive and reasonable. Whatever is not on the side of this "I" and "mine" we consider to be "other," and this we tend to meet with doubt and rejection.

What, then, is our greatest obstacle? Taking this precious "I" to be autonomous or independent. This type of conceptualizing is deeply lodged within our mind. How to break through it? We turn to the way of negation, and since we are investigating the view, we ask numerous questions. Does this "I" really exist? Or does it not exist? Turning these over and over in our minds, we become familiar with this "I"; we see that it is not possible to establish an independent "I" that does not rely on anything else. Investigating in this way weakens the habit of clinging to an "I." To the extent that this fixation decreases, so will all our other ways of grasping. And this allows us to continue looking for the abiding nature of things. As we do this, we will discover that this true nature falls into neither extreme of permanence or nihilism. Continuing our investigation, we come closer to mind's natural state, and our powers of insight grow. If we can reach a stable view, then it becomes possible for someone to point out the nature of our mind based upon view.

We are joyful then because we have found a view that transcends the world through a mind that is moving ever closer to seeing the abiding nature of things. It is like the meeting of a mother and child; they reach out to each other and touch hands: the mind that grasps on to "I" comes to be embraced by the wisdom that realizes no self.

This Life Is the Example

Now it is the afternoon and no doubt everyone is feeling a little drowsy, myself included. What we need to know is why this grasping on to a self is so powerful. The reason is it allows us to think that anger is all right if whatever is happening does not fit with the interests of "I" and "mine." Or, on the other hand, if it does fit, we think that whatever it is must be the best. What is the reason for this great attachment to ourselves? We could say that it comes from the habitual patterns of many lifetimes, but we cannot really know. What we can know is this life, and even from all these years, we do not remember many things, especially what was not so pleasant. I have forgotten much from my childhood. Of the many things that happened, I remember some, and usually what was nice. Those that were not so nice, I have mostly forgotten. Nevertheless, it is best to look at this life to find out how clinging to ourselves came about.

I would like to tell you a story about something that happened in my life, because I think that the strength of our grasping on to a self may depend on our childhood—how we were trained when we were young and how our parents brought us up. I remember that when I was very small, about three or four years old, my parents tried to bring me up well and loved me, which is the most important. All that they wanted was to give me whatever made me feel happy and loved. This is a very nice way to raise a child, but it also presents opportunities for pride to develop.

With this kind of upbringing, whenever some little thing does not go right, a child cries, and the parents immediately respond by trying to do something about it. The parents make an effort to find something that will please the child and give it to them, but they do not explain what they are doing and all the effort they went through. They just give the child what it wants, so the child becomes a little monarch, thinking, "Whatever I want and like happens. Whatever I don't like and don't want doesn't happen." As a result, even if the child does not feel self-important in the beginning, some arrogance develops. So in this situation, it is important to give an explanation that opens another perspective. The parents can make it clear to the child that in order to give something it liked, they had to go to a lot of trouble, which included eliminating all the things that the child did not like. If the child clearly understands the reasons why something positive happened, this could help to prevent a strong pride from developing.

During autumn in Tibet, animals are killed for their meat. As a young child I did not like this at all. Maybe there was some compassion involved, or maybe fear, but mostly I did not like to see animals being killed. I used to cry and say, "Don't kill them!" I would do different things to stop the slaughter but with no success. In our part of Tibet an animal is not killed with a knife but by suffocation, which involves tying up the animal's mouth and legs. When I saw this happening, I wanted to run there and take away all the bonds. But I was too small to untie them, so instead I would make a big scene by crying. But no matter what I did, I could not prevent what I did not want to happen.

Since they could not follow my wishes, my parents explained to me, "We can't follow your wishes. If we didn't kill this animal, we'd have no food. There'd be nothing for you to eat." I did understand that the place my parents lived was very high and vegetables do not grow, so there was nothing else to eat. Turning to Dharma, they also explained the killing from the standpoint of karma. Given our situation, we had no choice, for we were not independent of our karma. Hearing their explanations and reasons helped. I somewhat understood that the killing was done out of a need to survive and that karma played a role. This explanation of karma, however, did not make me happy. Seeing all the reasons why living beings are not independent and why they suffer gave me an even greater reason to be sad. Nevertheless, it is important to use such occasions to teach children on the spot so that when similar situations arise in the future, they can turn to their parents' explanation and understand more clearly. This was certainly beneficial for me, and maybe it can help others as well.

Parents do seek to create a wonderful world for their children, but even more splendid is to give them explanations that increase their intelligence and ability to discriminate right from wrong. In Buddhism, we speak of what is to be given up and what is to be taken up. According to the Dharma, what is most difficult to give up, even if we try very hard, is our ego-fixation, this grasping on to "I." Therefore, we are guiding our children in the wrong direction if we encourage their self-centeredness. We should teach them what is really useful. For example, parents might grow vegetables and give them to their child. This will help the child temporarily, but not as much as if they actually taught the child how to grow food. In the same way, as Dharma practitioners, especially those who are teachers, we have to take care that in explaining the Dharma to others, we help them understand in a practical and effective way and not one that will reinforce clinging to self.

Mistaking Emptiness

When we talk about emptiness, we do not mean a blank emptiness, a vacuum with nothing there—no causes, no effects, no
interdependence. This is the extreme of nihilism. If we think of
emptiness in this way, it can be very frightening. One day, when
I was around eight or nine years old, I was reading a text while
my teacher was sitting next to me. I was supposed to be studying, but thoughts were crowding around in my mind. I was not
thinking about emptiness, as I had not yet studied the major
texts on emptiness and compassion. I was thinking that people
died and that once the world has arisen, it ceases, even the
deities disappear. As I was imagining these end times, everything
vanished all around me. Even objects before my eyes melted
away like water. If I looked, nothing was clear. I was so terrified
that I began sweating and could not sit still, so I asked my
teacher if I could go outside. Not happy with this, he frowned
but did allow me to leave. I ran onto the flat roof next to my
rooms and walked back and forth while taking deep breaths,
and this did help. I think that if I had not gone outside at that
time, I might have gone mad. It was extremely scary.

This example shows that if we misunderstand emptiness to
be a blank nothingness, difficult experiences can happen. Later,
when I talked about it with another teacher, he said that what
had happened was good: "You were about to realize emptiness."
I am not sure whether that was the case or not. I do know that
thinking about emptiness as a void can engender a great deal of
fear. Consider all the suffering we experience when we do not
find the thing we want. How would we feel if every single thing
just vanished? The suffering and fear would be limitless.

So we can say that all phenomena are "empty," but we need
an explanation for this. We can say that there are "appearances,"
but we need to know how they exist and how to analyze the

diverse presentations of the way they arise. It is not enough to say that there is emptiness and there is appearance, or that something is just appearing over there. We need to know the nonduality of appearance and emptiness, the true nature of mind. This brings us back to the first verse of our text. Inseparable from our lama, Chenrezik has realized this nonduality, that which is most difficult to know. As the perfection of knowledge and love, these two are worthy of our greatest respect, and thus we pay homage to them.

CHAPTER 5

Turning to the Text

I T IS IMPORTANT to understand how to listen to the teaching and also how to understand the motivations and intentions of the master who wrote it. It is said, for example, that when Thogme Zangpo was writing this text, he did not have enough food to eat or good clothes to wear; he was, in fact, very poor. He first gave these teachings to some of his closest students, and from that time onward it is said that material resources came to him in a spontaneous way.

The Thirty-Seven Practices of a Bodhisattva is quite short. The words are few, but the meaning is profound, and though condensed, its instructions are comprehensive and practical—we can actually use them in our daily lives. All the topics presented in the text have a sound basis in the sutras, tantras, and authentic treatises. Further, the advice Thogme Zangpo gives is not simply what we might like to know, but what is valuable and relevant to the core practices of Buddhism. In sum, complete within *The Thirty-Seven Practices* are both the vast and the profound dimensions of the teachings. This is why so many have studied it and adopted these instructions as they traveled along the path of practice.

If we actually count the stanzas in the text, we will find forty-three, not thirty-seven. The first stanza is the homage, and the second, beginning with "Perfect buddhas, source of all benefit and happiness," is the promise to compose *The Thirty-Seven Practices*. These two beginning stanzas are not included in the thirty-seven because they are not instructions. The last four stanzas in the text, starting with "Following the meaning of the sutras and treatises," are also not counted because they are the concluding stanzas. So the actual instructions are only thirty-seven.

In the tradition of Buddhist writing, an author begins by paying homage to enlightened beings and follows it with verses that explain the title, give praise, and state a commitment to writing the text. The title of the text relates to how we engage in a bodhisattva's way of life. It is said that an authentic text is virtuous in the beginning because it gives the reason for creating the text, virtuous in the middle because it reveals the meaning of the main body of the text, and virtuous in the end because it summarizes the meaning in a conclusion. For beginning bodhisattvas, the path and advice on how to travel along it are explained gradually, and since the practices are condensed into thirty-seven and set in verse, the text is called *The Thirty-Seven Practices of a Bodhisattva*.

Homage

Namo Lokeshvaraya.
Seeing that all phenomena neither come nor go
Yet seeking only to benefit living beings,
The supreme master and the Protector Chenrezik
I honor continually with body, speech, and mind.

This opening stanza begins with the salutation *Namo Lokeshvaraya*, which means "to pay homage, or make a prostration, to our own special refuge." In Sanskrit, *namo* means "to pay homage," *loka* means "the world," and *ishvara* means "Lord." In this case, "Lord of the World" is another name for Avalokiteshvara, or Chenrezik in Tibetan. So the salutation simply means, "I pay homage to Avalokiteshvara." This homage and the following stanza are closely connected to the subject matter of the entire text, since they give the condensed meaning of the teachings on both wisdom and skillful means.

The first line, "Seeing that all phenomena neither come nor go," concerns omniscient wisdom. The ability to know belongs to the nature of the mind, so it is something that we all have; however, as we are now, we do not know everything. We do not know all objects of knowledge, because certain conditions obscure our knowing. Nevertheless, these obscurations are not part of mind's nature; they are obscurations to the mind and not a quality of the mind. If they belonged to the very basis of what mind is, they could not be cleared away. But we know that an obscuration is something that can be removed. For example, it is said that stripes are a quality of the tiger: the tiger would not be a tiger if it did not have stripes. The obscurations covering our mind, however, are not like this: they are not part of the nature of mind, for the mind has the quality of being clear and knowing. And obscurations have the quality of being able to be purified: since they do not belong to the nature of mind, they can be cleared away.

This indicates that an antidote could be used to work with the obscurations, and indeed there are certain methods that can be very effective. The more we work with them and the more these veils are lifted off, the stronger our knowing becomes. When all of the obscurations and impurities have been eradicated, our mind can know everything. It will clearly understand

and fully experience the whole range of phenomena, every object of awareness.

For various reasons, we place an object of knowledge into many different categories such as afflictive or nonafflictive, compounded or uncompounded. Depending on whether it is harmful or beneficial, we also define it as part of samsara or nirvana. In general, it is possible to describe the nature of a phenomenon in two different ways: in terms of how it truly is in its ultimate nature and as part of the whole range of phenomena that appear to us. When we talk about the whole range of phenomena, we mean anything that appears, or anything that is possible to be experienced by a consciousness.

It is important to understand that these two ways—the experience of a phenomenon and its nature—are the same thing, even though we may define it in two different ways. The way that all phenomena appear to our mind and the way they actually are may be defined differently, but the ultimate understanding is that the enlightened mind sees everything, both how phenomena appear and their true nature. We call Buddha's mind omniscient because it can be aware of everything. This means that the enlightened mind is completely conscious; it is able to see exactly the way the things are without obstruction or defilement. This is called enlightened mind or enlightened wisdom. Therefore, in the first stanza of The Thirty-Seven Practices, "Seeing that all phenomena neither come nor go" refers to the omniscient wisdom of a buddha.

In this way of looking with the wisdom of an enlightened mind—in other words, from the ultimate point of view or from the perspective of mind's nature—the whole range of phenomena of samsara and nirvana have the same taste; samsara and nirvana are seen to be equal. In Nagarjuna's Fundamentals of the Middle Way, this realization is brought about through negation. In the beginning of this famous text we find:

Whatever arises in dependence
Has no cessation and no arising
No extinction and no permanence
No coming or going,
And is neither different nor the same.
Mental constructs completely stilled,
It is taught to be peace.
I bow down to the genuine words
Of the perfect buddhas.

In the Madhyamaka teachings, it is said that to look at things without investigation or analysis is the samsaric way of seeing. With an untrained or unpurified mind, we see everything as separated by a dualistic focus into good and bad, inside and outside, and so forth. But when we look at the nature of things clearly and directly with full awareness, things are not as they appear. At this level of understanding or experience, which is beyond coming and going, phenomena do not really exist; they are seen to be free of any basis. People do not "go into" or "get out" of samsara, nor do they "go into" nirvana. Still, for an obscured state of mind, these things seem to happen.

Emptiness and Compassion

Enlightened persons, who see all of this clearly, become so filled with compassion that their sole desire is to help others. They have no other purpose or activity except to work for the benefit of those caught in samsara, who still do not understand phenomena as they truly are. When the level of realization beyond coming and going is attained, a person is a bodhisattva or a buddha, able to appear in a variety of forms. To help people whose minds need subduing, they appear in a wrathful form. For those who need to work with attachment, they take the appropriate form. For those who are dealing with anger and hatred, they appear in yet another form that is relevant to this situation. In this way buddhas and bodhisattvas manifest myriad forms. Chenrezik is a bodhisattva known for love and compassion. He radiates these qualities and, through them, works for the welfare of sentient beings. This is why the first stanza honors the supreme master and the Protector Chenrezik, for they are inseparable.

There is a story related to our text that illustrates why it is sometimes necessary for buddhas or bodhisattvas to take on different forms in order to help others. It is said that very long ago, during the time of another buddha named Kashyapa, the First Karmapa was ordained. At that time he said to another monk, "You look like a monkey." For this remark, it is said that during his next five hundred lives he was reborn as a monkey. Many years later, when this monk became the First Karmapa, Dusum Khyenpa, he was not very handsome since he looked a little like a monkey. It seems that before becoming a monk, he had a girlfriend, who left him because he was not good-looking. When that happened, he was so saddened that he became a renunciate, entered the monastery, and devoted himself to Dharma practice. Afterward, having attained realization, he thought, "If I have this unattractive form in the future, I don't think I'll be able to help other beings. My face will just turn them away." Therefore he prayed with compassion, "In the future, may I always have a nice-looking face."

A teacher's compassion, which opens the door to Dharma, can take many forms. It is said that for some people, no amount of teaching will help. They will not get anything from a lot of talking and will need something else. So sometimes by manifesting a special appearance or an inspiring way of being, one can help them transform. Sometimes a mind-to-mind connection will help. The true teacher is flexible in finding what fits the student.

Promise to Compose

Perfect buddhas, source of all benefit and happiness,
Arise through accomplishing the genuine Dharma;
Since this in turn depends on knowing how to practice,
The practices of a bodhisattva will be explained.

This verse represents a promise to compose the text. The first line, stating that perfect buddhas are the "source of all benefit and happiness" has to be understood correctly. What the text means is that happiness and well-being are the result of positive deeds, and the Dharma as taught by the buddhas shows us which deeds are positive and which are not. Therefore, if we practice following these instructions, we will achieve happiness and be able to benefit others. Sometimes people make the mistake of thinking that all their happiness depends directly on the Buddha or the lama. They regard these teachers as all-powerful while thinking that they themselves can do very little or even nothing at all. Praying to others, they ask, "Please make me happy. Make everything go well." However, to believe that the buddhas are omnipotent and to depend on them as if our happiness can be willed by them is not the way. The buddhas do not have the power to give us happiness. After all, if they did have such power, there would be no problems in the world, would there? But in fact, our happiness depends on us. We have to create it: no one else can give it to us. So we need to know how to engender our own happiness deep within, and this is what the buddhas teach. It is extremely important to understand this.

How do we create our happiness? We work on our motivation and our actions, and to do that, we should know how to practice Dharma. We train in being careful and mindful, aware of what is to be done and what is not to be done. The benefits that "arise through accomplishing the genuine Dharma" do not just happen, nor does becoming a buddha just happen. Like a ripening fruit, the Buddha matured over time into full awakening. In the same way, we also have to work with the Dharma and practice it, because we do not become enlightened without any reason, without any causes or conditions.

It is said that compassion is the root cause of enlightenment. Without compassion, it is not possible to become enlightened, so our compassion is crucial. Bodhichitta is the main element in Dharma practice, and the six paramitas are regarded as the method to develop it. The buddhas and bodhisattvas are always engaging in these in order to train their minds, and we should follow their example. The practices of a bodhisattva explained in this text set in motion the causes and conditions that will lead us to full awakening.

CHAPTER 6

What Is Genuine Practice?

1

Now that we have a vessel of leisure and resources, so
difficult to find,
So that we may bring ourselves and others across the
ocean of samsara,
Without a break during day or night
To listen, reflect, and meditate is the practice of a
bodhisattva.

THE FIRST INSTRUCTION in *The Thirty-Seven Practices of a Bodhisattva* is about how to practice Dharma. In the beginning, we must have the desire to practice, and then we listen or study in order to develop our understanding. Yet understanding is not enough. We also need confidence, a kind of certainty, and for this, reflection is necessary. Gaining confidence in the teachings and the practice of Dharma is also not enough. We have to blend it with our way of experiencing, and to do that, meditation is necessary. Therefore to practice the Dharma, we need to do three things: study, reflect, and meditate.

The text states that since we have a very precious human body, now is the time we can practice Dharma. And to do this well, we need to know what to cultivate and what to eliminate from among all the things we usually do. Without the capacity to do certain things and abstain from others, we are not free to practice. But human beings do have this capacity and that is why a human life is the most suitable one for the practice of Dharma. We can see that some animals have very special qualities and some can do unusual things. But it may not be possible for them consciously and consistently to engage one thing and abstain from another as human beings can, so animals are not really free to practice. As human beings, we have this special chance, a special freedom, so we need to work diligently and wholeheartedly, both day and night.

It is not enough to listen to the teachings with interest and attention. Even when we are not listening to teachings, we should keep our mind on the Dharma so that whatever arises in our mind blends together with it. When we can do this, we are truly practicing. The text states that we should practice day and night without becoming distracted. How do we do that? How to practice so that our mind doesn't stray? To answer this, we need to know what constitutes the unmistaken practice of Dharma.

The Kadampas have a story about someone who wanted to practice the Dharma. He did not know how to practice, so at first he tried in a mistaken way, and only later did he find out what real practice is all about. The young man started by circumambulating a stupa. Not looking here and there, he very diligently went around and around many times. He did this earnestly for a long while. Eventually, along came a great Kadampa master, who saw him and asked, "What are you doing here?"

The young man said, "I'm practicing Dharma. I'm circumambulating the stupa."

The Kadampa master replied, "You're circumambulating.

That's very good. But wouldn't it be better to do genuine Dharma practice?" The Kadampa master then went away, leaving the young man perplexed.

He said to himself, "I thought I was practicing Dharma, but maybe this is not it. What, then, is Dharma practice?" He decided that reading scriptures must be the way. He went to the library, took out some books, and began reading. He was reading with great dedication and reciting the scriptures, when again he met the Kadampa master.

Once more the master asked, "What are you doing?"

The practitioner said, "I'm reading scriptures and practicing Dharma."

The master replied, "That's very good. But wouldn't it be better for you to engage in genuine Dharma practice?"

Now the young man was quite confused, and he did not know what to do. So he thought about it and finally exclaimed, "That's it! Meditation! It's nothing more than that." So he went to a quiet corner and sat with his legs crossed, closed his eyes, and meditated, thinking that he was doing great practice.

But again the Kadampa master appeared and asked, "What are you doing here?"

"I'm practicing Dharma and meditating."

The master said, "It is very good to do some meditation. But wouldn't it be better if you really practiced the Dharma free of error?"

Now the practitioner was totally confounded, and asked, "What is real Dharma practice, then? It's not circumambulating the stupa. It's not reading scriptures. It's not meditating. What is it?"

The Kadampa master replied, "Cut through your attachment. That is the practice of Dharma."

Like the person in this story, many people want to practice, and they take up the preliminary practices of the ngondro. If we ask people what they did and what was the result of their practice, some will say, "Oh, it was very difficult when I did the prostrations. I sweated off a few pounds." These people will talk about how much effort they made and what difficulties and problems they had. If the result of their practice was even better, they might say, "Oh, it was great! It was so beautiful!" and they will talk about all the good feelings they had.

Then there are people who want to talk about an even higher attainment. They will say, "Oh, I had an incredible experience! I saw Vajrayogini dancing in front of me!" These people will claim to see deities and have other special experiences. As a result, we may think that these signs are the results of practice, and since they happen to some people, they will happen for us as well. But these are not really the important results.

We all know that when we practice a lot and become a bit tired or upset, we can become unbalanced, and then all sorts of seemingly positive or negative things can appear in our mind. These are not necessarily the real signs of practice. The real sign of our practice should be how we work with our afflicting emotions. For example, we could recall, "Yesterday at nine o'clock someone did something awful to me and I was about to get angry, but then I reflected on it and didn't get angry." This kind of result shows whether or not our practice has actually become the antidote to our negative feelings and thoughts. This is very important, because sometimes we do not see what Dharma practice actually is and what it is really for. We do some practice, but we take another kind of outcome as the real result. This is a mistake we should not make.

Beyond Separation

Sometimes we talk about practicing the Dharma as if it were something to be done. We see our mind as one thing and Dharma practice as another: our mind is here while Dharma practice is over there. This is not true Dharma practice. When we talk about love and compassion, for example, we could think, "I have to generate love and compassion," as if we have to bring them in from someplace else, as if our mind as it is cannot be love at that very moment. If we want to generate bodhichitta, it is this mind that we have right now that we should allow to arise as love and compassion. Compassion is not somewhere else: it is our present mind that is compassionate. Dharma practice is not something we do while our mind is elsewhere. If that were the case, our practice could not have a transformative effect on our mind. So this separation is the problem, whether we are trying to generate love and compassion or trying to work on our negative emotions. It is the same in every case: it has to happen in our mind, which, as it arises, is inseparable from love and compassion. When this happens, we are truly practicing Dharma.

It is important to distinguish between a meditation session and the time afterward. During the session, we completely concentrate on what we are doing, whether it is analyzing something or letting our mind settle into a meditative state. There is a saying in Tibetan that flesh and bones get mixed together; in other words, we become completely one with the practice. When the session finishes and the postsession period begins, the practice no longer occupies our mind completely. Nevertheless, we try to maintain some beneficial effect from the meditative state. Before we stop the session, we should make this intention: "After I finish this session, throughout the rest of the day I will try to retain the flavor of this experience and state of mind."

In this way, although our mind is not as intently focused as it is during a session of practice, we are still living within the effect. These two phases reinforce each other. The practice session influences our whole day, and the way we live the entire day also helps to make the actual practice session more powerful and meaningful.

How do we practice at night? Obviously, we cannot have a session and then move into postsession. If we think too much before we sleep, we might not get to sleep at all. It is said that the sleep turns into whatever our state of our mind was just before we fell asleep. If our mental state was positive, sleep becomes positive; if it was negative, sleep becomes negative. When we are lying in bed at night, before we actually fall asleep, many of us think about what we have done during the day and plan what we are going to do tomorrow. We could take this time to sort out what we did during the day. What was virtuous and what was not? When we have separated one from the other, we can make a commitment that the next day we will try to increase positive actions and decrease negative ones. With that motivation, the whole night can turn into a positive practice. If we can go to sleep in this way, our sleep will not be useless or without purpose; it will turn into a positive state of mind, and thereby the power of what is virtuous will increase.

This ends the first stanza of the thirty-seven practices, and now we need to move along. This is the twenty-first century and we should not get stuck in one place. We should go forward like a nice big car.

CHAPTER 7
Exploring the Familiar

2

> Attachment to friends churns like water;
> Aversion to enemies burns like fire.
> Dark with ignorance—not knowing what to adopt or
>   reject—
> To give up this homeland is the practice of a bodhisattva.

WHEN PEOPLE ARE CLOSE to us and material things are nearby, what often appear are attachment and its opposite, aversion. When we become familiar with something that seems nice and agreeable, suited to our way of thinking, we become attached to it. If something bad happens to people or things connected with us, our mind becomes disturbed. This is easy to understand; however, it is also true that familiarity is also needed for aversion to arise. We cannot consider someone an enemy if we know nothing about her or him, because to say someone is bad, we need to know why. We count up all the negative things about someone before we see this person as our enemy, and therefore, even to have an enemy, we need a certain familiarity. When we conclude that something is not nice or does not suit us, we see it as an enemy, setting it apart and developing an aversion to it. So both attachment and aversion stem from being familiar with their objects.

It is usually understood that familiarity happens when we are in the same place for a long time, and that is the way the Tibetan word *pha yul*, or "homeland," is used in this text. For example, I have left Tibet, but that does not mean that I have no aversion or attachment. When we talk about "homeland" as it is used here, we are not just talking about a home or a land; we are talking about a situation that serves to increase our aversion or attachment. Therefore, the main instruction is to lighten the strong attachment and aversion that weigh on our mind.

However close we may be to a friend or however much we may think we know about a person, it is possible that we will find out something—a secret, a problem, or a mistake—that we did not know before. However good this friend may seem, he or she may have concealed faults and problems. By contrast, we may see nothing good in our enemy and think this person is just a heap of faults. Yet however great our dislike may be, we could discover something we did not know. There may be some reason for being like that; for example, a situation, over which a person had no control, could have led him or her to behave badly. After all, if there was no reason for the person to be so negative, he or she would not have become our enemy.

It is better, therefore, not to look at friends or enemies from an extreme point of view—seeing a friend as completely good and an enemy as completely evil. Even though it may not be possible right now to view enemies and friends as equals, we should try to understand and react in a way that is not excessive: our friend is not one hundred percent right and our enemy not one hundred percent wrong. This is the real subject of this second instruction. It is not about abandoning our country; our place of residence is not what primarily determines the way we react. Even Thogme Zangpo would say he is from Tibet. The instructions are not about getting rid of our home or leaving our land; they concern avoiding extremes of attachment and aversion when relating to our "friends" and "enemies."

CHAPTER 8

Letting Go of Worldly Concerns

3

By leaving harmful places, afflictions gradually decline.
With no distractions, virtuous activity naturally grows.
With a clear mind, certainty in the Dharma arises.
To rely on solitude is the practice of a bodhisattva.

SOLITUDE IS EXTREMELY IMPORTANT, especially for calm abiding or shamatha meditation. It is usually said that if we find a nice solitary place and practice well for about three to five months, we will achieve calm abiding. It is sometimes even said that if we do not attain it within this time, we will not attain it at all, but that may not be completely true. For me personally, this kind of outer solitude is over with. The most solitude that I have is my own room, and even then there is not so much.

What is real solitude? It can be divided into inner and outer solitude. Whatever our personal situation may be, whether we live alone or with others, outer solitude is not enough, because it is something external, "out there," like a time when there is no crowd around us. But actually, outer solitude is not as important as inner solitude, since all disturbances come from within. Therefore, it is more difficult to find inner solitude. We create our own crowd of thoughts that jostle our mind. Since they are within us, these distractions are not easily banished. Though difficult to find, inner solitude is the most important thing; outer solitude alone is not enough. Please try to find real solitude.

4

> Everyone will part from relatives and old friends;
> The wealth of long labor will be left behind;
> The guest, consciousness, leaves its lodging, the body,
>   behind:
> To give up concern for this life is the practice of a
>   bodhisattva.

It is said that whether our Dharma practice is effective or not depends on whether we can give up our concern for this life, which is often described in terms of the eight worldly dharmas, (concerns about gain and loss, pleasure and pain, fame and oblivion, praise and blame). And it is during this life that we have the opportunity to work with them. We should not procrastinate and think that we will do it later in this or another life. In a key text of the Sakya tradition, *Cutting Free of the Four Attachments*, it is said that if we are attached to this life, we are not a genuine Dharma practitioner. The true Dharma practitioner is free of clinging to this existence.

When we talk about this life's concerns (summarized by the eight worldly dharmas), we should understand why we need to work on giving them up. The reason is that they represent our attachments, the various ways we cling to all the things of this world. It does not matter whether these things seem to be nice or unpleasant, good or bad, beneficial or harmful. It is just our clinging to them—blindly without understanding or thinking—that disturbs our mind and fills us with apprehension.

Many of us like the Dharma and want to practice it. But often we practice seriously when we are unhappy and have some problems, so actually we are just trying to make ourselves happier. When we have back pain, we apply gels and get a massage, and then we feel a bit better. Our Dharma practice is a little like this. We think that it is something to do when there is a problem, but our main attraction is to this life, to the world and all of its entertainments. We consider our worldly possessions crucial to our lives, the very source of our happiness. Even if we do not think like this consciously, in the background of our mind, our unconscious attitude holds on to all these worldly things as if our happiness truly depended on them.

When we have this attitude, our Dharma practice starts to resemble the treatment of AIDS. I've been told that when one has AIDS, the food one eats first feeds the AIDS virus and only afterward, when the virus is satiated, does it go to the parts of our body that are healthy. Something like this happens when we practice Dharma with too much attachment to the eight worldly concerns. Like the AIDS virus, they receive most of our attention, while the Dharma is second in line. Another example is that of our mind as a screen. When we project a movie on the worldly side of the screen, we get a bright array of attractive images, but the Dharma side of the screen has nothing much on it. This is how we practice Dharma if our mind is preoccupied with mundane affairs.

Death Is Not the End

When looking at our lives, we need to see a continuum, a linkage from childhood to the present and on into the future. If we did not see any continuation from this life into the next, we would have no reason not to regard this life's interests as the most important. There are numerous discussions about whether there is an afterlife or not. Reasonable arguments can be made on both sides and no one can say definitively that it is this way or that. But one thing we have found. Suppose we have a friend or someone we love deeply and that person dies or disappears. Because of our love for this person, it is very difficult, in fact almost impossible, to feel that this person is totally gone and never present in some way.

Most people have a feeling that the loved one who has passed away is somehow still available. We talk to them in our mind, we visit the place where they were cremated or buried, and we offer flowers while praying for their well-being. We dream that he or she is still alive; some may even see or feel the presence of a person who has passed away. It is a natural thing. This feeling is not something that comes from religion. It is our love that leads us to believe that there is something naturally inborn that is not finished when we die. Whether we are thinking about ourselves or about others, we have a very strong feeling that there is something that does not end. We do not see ourselves as a candle that is finished when the last flame goes out, but as a torch, a light shining everywhere that can be transferred one bright flame to the next. I believe that this way of thinking is very important.

If we think that death is the end, we are filled with remorse and fear. But, to turn briefly to logic, if death is an end, then its cause must be birth, for we cannot have one without the other. In that case we should take birth to be as unfortunate as death and we would have to put a stop to all birthday celebrations. Seriously, however, we need not see death as the end, because death is a continuation of birth. Death is not nothingness or a blank state; it is the time when we transfer our light to another way of being. With this understanding, we can see that it is possible to dedicate our lives toward bringing light into the world for future generations as well as for our own future. If we can understand this, then death does not become an end, nor is it something to fear.

CHAPTER 9

Negative and Positive Friends

Make friends with these and the three poisons grow;
The activities of listening, reflecting, and meditating
    decline
While love and compassion are destroyed.
To cast off bad friends is the practice of a bodhisattva.

A S WE GO THROUGH LIFE, we depend on our friends, and these friends can be positive or negative. When a friend is negative, it means that when we associate with this person, some of our more positive and subtle habitual tendencies may be changed or destroyed. But this does not mean that through this friend, we become something completely different or that we are affected in an obviously negative way.

Further, when we talk about giving up negative friends, we are not necessarily talking about individual people; we can also be pointing to influences. On a deeper level, this verse is actually about our own mind and whether it is focused on positive things or turned toward negative ones. When our mind is involved with the three poisons (ignorance, aversion, and excessive desire), all our negative emotions expand, and their influence over us increases. Therefore, though we may try to avoid negative people, if our mind is unable to disconnect from our own poisons and inner negative influences, our practice will not go well.

6

> Rely on this one and defects disappear;
> Qualities increase like the waxing moon.
> To cherish a genuine spiritual friend
> More than our own body is the practice of a bodhisattva.

This verse speaks of a "good" friend, or positive influence, which we call a "spiritual friend." The literature of Buddhism discusses the many different qualities of a spiritual friend or teacher. From the Vinaya to the Vajrayana, a variety of spiritual characteristics are recommended, and it may not be easy to find someone who has them all. In fact, it is very difficult to find such a person. Nevertheless, we have to try to find someone who has fewer faults and weaknesses and more positive qualities.

The last two lines of this stanza tell us how to relate to this person, which is to "cherish a genuine spiritual friend more than our own body." It is important, however, that we do not make a mistake here but relate to our spiritual friend in a correct way. When we are searching for the right guide, it is said that we should not choose too soon and that we should stay focused on our purpose, not accepting just anyone we meet who is called a teacher. It is not necessary to take someone as a spiritual friend immediately. Nevertheless, once we have decided to relate to someone as our teacher, we should not continue to look around. In brief, we should search first and be very clear about our decision, and only then relate to someone as our spiritual friend.

Not choosing a spiritual friend too soon means that when we start searching, we consider whether a person has all, or most of, the qualities of a teacher. This is the focus of our investigation, not whether we like the person or not. If we are preoccupied with our likes and dislikes and do not examine someone's qualifications as a spiritual friend, we will not know whether we are attracted to a good person or a bad person, to someone who has the necessary qualities or not. We could like someone who does not measure up, and without knowing it, we could be relating to an unqualified person. For that reason, we should not be too hasty in choosing a spiritual friend.

Once we have accepted someone as our spiritual friend, however, we search no more. We should already have done whatever tests were necessary to find out whether the qualities of this potential teacher were greater than his or her faults, and at that point we should have made our decision. Having done this, we stop evaluating the teacher. At this point, there is no benefit in continuing to test, because now we have to relate to that person as our guide. How do we do this? We do not think, "The Buddha said it is good to have a spiritual friend, so I must have one." Here, it is not just our head but our feelings that come into play. This connection with a teacher has to come from our heart in a living way and to spring from our deepest aspiration. We relate with our whole being to discover how our practice can benefit from this relationship. "What do I have to learn?" "What is my real interest?" It is our experience that will give us the answer, not endless examination.

It is a little like loving someone. We do not love a person because we have been told that we must love them. We love someone because it flows from our heart. In the same way, relating to the spiritual friend has to come from our heart and resonate with our deepest purpose in life. When this happens, we receive the benefits of an authentic relationship with a spiritual friend. Otherwise, if we keep on examining, we will create a distance between ourselves and our teacher.

Further, since every human being has a positive side and a negative side, both qualities and faults, we will certainly find some faults; there is no human being who is free of every fault. If we find some faults in our new spiritual friend, we might seek out another teacher and begin anew with another chapter. Again we will go through the whole process of investigation and testing, and again we will find faults, so the process will just keep on repeating itself. We could spend our whole life trying to find the right spiritual friend and never receive any of the benefits this relationship has to offer.

CHAPTER 10

Going for Refuge

7

Captive themselves in the prison of samsara,
Whom could the worldly gods protect?
Therefore, when seeking protection, to go for refuge
To the unfailing Three Jewels is the practice of a
bodhisattva.

IN SOME COUNTRIES, there are ancient ways that are not necessarily part of an established religious or philosophical tradition, but belong to a kind of animism. If people see an
impressive rock, they think there is something special there. An
outstanding tree several hundred years old is thought to be extraordinary. This kind of worship relies on worldly gods, ele-
mental spirits, and so forth, which people see as being external
to themselves and at the same time very powerful. Not taking responsibility for their own future, people make prayers to these
spirits or beings, putting their whole life in another's hands.

To a certain extent, these practices can have a positive effect.

In Tibet people point to a mountain and say, "This mountain is such-and-such a god." The benefit of this is that it helps to protect the environment. If the mountain is sacred, it cannot be destroyed or harmed. In this way not only is the environment protected, but many animals living on the mountain are saved as well. When I was young, we children were told that there were deities and spirits in the mountains. When we went near these special places, we felt that we had to behave ourselves and not make too much noise. We had learned a certain principle or code that was beneficial to the land where we lived.

In Buddhism, however, our approach to seeking protection is different. We can understand what protection or refuge essentially is through the example of our daily lives. We can see that for the most part our parents have protected us from the time we were born. In Buddhism, we take this a step further and say that we ourselves are our own protectors. We are the ones who give ourselves refuge, for example, from suffering. When we die, we are the ones who must make the effort to maintain clarity and awareness without depending on anyone else. However, this is quite difficult, so in the beginning we rely on others.

What should this "other" be like? It should be someone who desires to benefit us and does not deceive. The Three Jewels—the Buddha (the teacher), the Dharma (the teachings), and the Sangha (the community)—are like this: they are stable and trustworthy. In taking refuge, we enter into a reciprocal relationship: the Three Jewels give us the protection of being a refuge, and we in turn give them our trust. When we go for refuge, we think of all Three Jewels, understanding that the Buddha is like a doctor, the Dharma is like his medicine, and the Sangha is like a nurse.

In general, there are four reasons to take refuge. One is to free ourselves from samsara; the second is to free others from their fears; the third is to develop compassion that is not attached to those who are close (friends and relatives) and so avoid feeling a separation from those who are far (enemies); and the fourth reason is that our compassion will grow and extend beyond the world that we know to all living beings. Seeing how the Buddha embodied all these qualities, we understand by implication that his teachings and those who follow them are precious, so we go for refuge to all three—the Buddha, the Dharma, and the Sangha.

Of the Three Jewels, however, the Dharma is considered most important. Sometimes, we have strange ideas about the Buddha. We go to him for refuge and then think that he will extend his large hand down from the sky and lift us out of samsara. Actually, the Buddha came into the world, taught the path to liberation, and then passed away. Since we cannot go looking for him now, what should we do? We can rely on the Dharma he bequeathed to us and practice as much as possible this path to full awakening. The Dharma is the Buddha's representative. If we put into practice the meaning of his words, it is the same as if the Buddha were present and we could see him and hear him teaching us. This is why the Dharma is so important.

The community of practitioners (*sangha* in Sanskrit) is known in Tibetan as *gendun*, which literally means "those who aspire to virtue." In the strict sense of the term, it refers to those who abide on the bodhisattva levels. In another sense, it refers to a gathering of a minimum of four monastics, because the Buddha has stated that when four are assembled, it is as if he himself were present. However, the term can also refer to our friends on the path. Friends are important, both in the mundane world and in the world of Dharma. I have heard that people make close connections on the battlefield and have war buddies. But our goals are different. Lifetime after lifetime, we are seeking the level of full awakening, and our friends are those who share our interests, who are involved in the deep questions of life just as we are. However, even if our excellent friends abide on bodhisattva levels, they will not benefit us if we do not know how to rely on our own deeper thoughts. Further, if we happen to have negative friends, through our kindness and intelligence, we can lead them to develop positive qualities without being affected by their faults.

Ultimately, we are our own refuge. This means that we are responsible for protecting ourselves, that no one else can do this. We ourselves must clearly understand what to take up and what to give up and then actually do it. This is the true practice of Dharma. It creates the causes and conditions for our happiness and, further, for attaining wisdom, compassion, and the ability to help others.

So we examine and then broaden our comprehension, cultivating within ourselves our own ways of being compassionate and wise. With method and wisdom in harmony, we develop the ability to work for the benefit of both ourselves and others. In this way, through our own effort we can protect ourselves and transcend suffering. As we have seen, we also depend on the Buddha, Dharma, and Sangha. But in the end, full awakening depends on us, because in the main, we are the ones responsible. Focused inward on our own minds, we watch carefully, learning what to discard and what to develop. This understanding is the root, the essence, of refuge.

CHAPTER 11

The Karma of Happiness and Suffering

8

The sufferings of the lower realms so difficult to bear
Come from misdeeds, thus the Buddha taught.
Therefore, even at the risk of our life,
Never to commit these actions is the practice of a
bodhisattva.

THIS STANZA IS ABOUT KARMA, or cause and effect. If our action is positive, its result will be positive. If our action is harmful, the result will be harmful. All actions produce their corresponding results in a similar way, because karma is action and reaction. Like water flowing down or smoke floating up, it is something natural, and we cannot argue about it or change the way it functions. Therefore, we should find out which causes are beneficial and which are harmful, and act accordingly.

The lower realms have been described as deep underneath us or far away from the earth. But we can find smaller versions of these realms in this very world, right before our eyes. It is not necessary to look below the earth or anywhere else, because war and famine are happening right now, and they are exactly what has been described as the misery of the lower realms. All of this suffering and pain comes from the terrible situations we know through personal experience or through the media. This is a fact. It is not something that I am saying to scare people or claiming to be true because it fits my way of thinking. Karma, or cause and effect, is a natural process, and it is one we should understand in depth.

For our own good, we learn what causes joy or pain and then follow this understanding into action. Practicing like this is not just for our own future benefit but also for the future of our children and all the generations to come. We must make a serious effort not to do anything that brings suffering and pain to ourselves or others, such as killing and war.

If we will refrain from negative actions—for example, the ten negative actions taught in Buddhism (killing, stealing, lying, and so forth)—we will naturally create an environment that will bring more happiness and more peace into each individual's life as well as to entire countries and then the whole world.

9

Happiness in the three realms is like dew on a
    blade of grass—
Its nature is to evaporate in an instant.
To strive for the supreme state of liberation
That never changes is the practice of a bodhisattva.

Understanding the impermanence of all phenomena in the three realms (the desire realm, the form realm, and the formless realm) impels us toward liberation. It is crucial for us to understand that liberation has everything to do with our mind. External things—outer happiness and suffering or the conditions

that bring them about—cannot be easily changed. Our body
and external things are always limited. For example, we could
train in a sport such as the long jump, and we could get better
and better at it, but there is a boundary: we cannot go beyond
the physical limits of the body. The mind, however, is free from
such limitations, and its power can develop continuously. If we
are trying to make this life better, but limit the progress that we
can make within our mind, that would be very sad, even de-
pressing. Our perspective and our vision should be limitless so
that our mind can evolve and attain liberation, which is vast
and beyond measure.

10

From time beyond time, our mothers have cared for us;
If they suffer, what good is our own happiness?
Thus, to liberate living beings beyond number,
To engender bodhichitta is the practice of a bodhisattva.

Sometimes we think that if we had lots of money, we would be
perfectly happy. But we all know that this is not the case. Even
when we have money, happiness and satisfaction do not come
so easily. Once I saw a documentary about a small girl who
needed to have blood transfusions, but her family did not have
the money to pay for them. So all of her school friends, who
were young children, helped by selling their toys. Whatever precious ones they had—teddy bears, dolls, or stuffed animals—
they sold and gave all the money to help her.

Now, children have very strong feelings about their toys. I
even heard that once, when a family's house was collapsing, a
child ran back in to get his favorite toy. When these school-
children sacrificed their own toys to collect money for their
friend, it was not a small thing. Although materially it might
not have amounted to much, for them it was huge. As I watched
this film, I was thinking that I could give a donation. But if I

did, I would feel ashamed, for even if I gave many millions, compared to the gifts that the children gave from their heart with so much love and sacrifice, my gift would not amount to anything.

This verse underlines the importance of knowing that real satisfaction does not come from having an easy life and plenty of money. These days I have a fairly comfortable life, even peace of mind, but that alone does not give me the greatest satisfaction. Real satisfaction comes when I can do something that really helps someone else without any hope of getting something in return, such as fame or a good reputation. The chance to give people something that truly benefits them does bring the greatest satisfaction.

CHAPTER 12

Exchanging Self for Other

11

All suffering comes from wanting happiness for ourselves;
Perfect buddhas arise from the intention to benefit others.
Therefore, to truly exchange our happiness
For the suffering of others is the practice of a bodhisattva.

THIS STANZA IS ABOUT exchanging whatever we have that is positive for whatever others have that is not. Why is it true that all the suffering in the world comes from wishing happiness for ourselves alone? If we concentrate only on our own comfort and happiness, we become self-centered and arrogant, and sooner or later this leads to suffering. This much is clear to us all.

But when we say that wishing happiness for others brings us happiness, what do we mean by "other"? An obvious answer is all living beings who are not ourselves. We can also observe that life cannot possibly go on without the flow of giving and taking among all these forms of life. Our own breathing is an example of this. What we exhale is good for some other living things, and in turn what they exhale is good for us. There are numerous ways that living beings depend on one another. We know this intellectually, but do not understand it in a practical, experiential way. And when we do not actually live our lives with this expansive sense of give and take, our practice becomes the opposite of what we think we believe; for example, it runs counter to our ideas of interdependence or benefiting others. Furthermore, our holding back from giving keeps us from receiving.

We may talk about the equality of ourselves and others, or exchanging ourselves with others, but we do not understand that this happens in everyday life. We think that it is something special or extraordinary, yet it is happening in our lives on a daily basis. We give something, and that opens the possibility of receiving: we naturally receive something when we give. This is how we live, whether it is in the business world, in our social lives, or in any other context. Giving and taking is happening all the time. Living is dependent on giving: we give and therefore we receive. This interdependence is natural; however, it takes a special effort to train our mind to know this well enough so that our understanding is clear and strong.

It is cherishing ourselves that blocks this knowing. When something good occurs, we may think, "This is happening because of me. It's all due to my talent and energy." This makes "me" way too important. This is not to say that we should not do something for ourselves or that we do not have to care for ourselves. Of course, we have to take care of ourselves, but it should not be in an extreme way—caring for ourselves alone and attaching too much importance to our own aims and desires. If we think, "I'm the top priority. They are farther down the line," that is a problem. We need to practice letting others come to the fore and letting ourselves melt into the background.

The Actual Practice

The meditation practice of sending and receiving (*tonglen*) is a way to reverse cherishing ourselves. The practice of giving and taking puts less emphasis on our own interests and gives greater priority to the interests of others. As we meditate, we exhale, giving out everything positive we have, and inhale, taking on everything negative from others. For example, to start this practice, we might visualize others who are in difficult situations or place a photograph of people who are sick in front of us. A common way of practicing tonglen is to take in the disease, pain, or problems of a person who is in difficulty. Through our two nostrils we breathe in these negative aspects as a black cloud or a very dark and murky solution.

Some of us might think that if we are taking from someone who has a knee pain, for example, we would almost feel that pain in our knee. If we are taking from someone who has a headache or problem in their brain, we would feel a little uneasiness in our own head. This is often considered to be authentic tonglen practice. However, this is not necessarily the right kind of practice, because the exchange of our happiness for other's suffering is not about giving pain to our body or problems to ourselves. The point of the practice is to diminish clinging to ourselves. So it is not that we attack or harm our own well-being—this is not really tonglen practice.

We might say that the actual practice starts with viewing our mind as if it had two parts. One part thinks, "I want to be happy and want others to be happy, too." This is the reasonable part of our mind. But there is another part that thinks, "I'm the only one. It's just me that needs happiness and well-being." This part is all about "I," "me," and "myself alone." It is the part of our mind that we need to work on.

There are many other ways to do this visualization. One is to imagine a candle as the negative aspects of our mind, such as being self-centered. Everything negative is absorbed into the flame. Through practicing over time, this self-cherishing state of mind is diminished and eventually eliminated. This process will not affect us in a negative way; it only affects our self-absorption, the mistaken way of grasping on to ourselves. The self-cherishing "I" that we visualized as a candle was created by our imagination, so we are not actually harming ourselves but still working on reducing our ego-fixation.

Furthermore, according to traditional logic, this self-centered, autonomous "I" does not truly exist, because an "I" can only exist in relationship to something else, for example, another person or an object, so this "I" is not independent and unitary. It is impossible for an isolated "I" to truly exist; it is only present in dependence on something else.

Through this practice of exchange, we come to see that self and other are equal; our interest and that of others are equal. We make a strong aspiration prayer that others receive everything positive that we have, whatever it may be—long life, riches, power, and so forth. We wish all of this for others and feel that they receive it. This kind of meditative training benefits both ourselves and others. It is important to understand that it is not the case that our positive qualities, such as the length of our life or our positive energy, are carried over like some object and given to others, nor are these positive qualities ever exhausted, because they belong to who we truly are.

Wishing something good for others and making dedications for their benefit come from a powerful wish that is based on a positive motivation. This is why others might receive something while we do not lose anything. Indeed, there are many reasons to believe that others do get some benefit out of this, and that is why tonglen is a very important practice. However, the main reason for this practice is to reduce our own selfish concerns and to increase our intention to wish others well. This is the real focus of the practice.

CHAPTER 13

Dealing with Adversity

12

If out of great desire someone steals all our wealth
Or makes another do so,
To dedicate our body, possessions, and all merit of the
     three times
To this person is the practice of a bodhisattva.

I F ALL OUR POSSESSIONS WERE STOLEN, we would naturally call the police. Nothing else would come to mind. But there is another way to deal with it, as this story about a robbery in Tibet shows. It comes from Lhathok, the area of my home in Eastern Tibet.

A man from Lhathok was traveling in his home territory when robbers fell upon him and stole everything he had, including his horse. There was nothing left but a cup with a silver lining, which he kept in his inner pouch. As the robbers were about to leave, the man took out this cup and said to the robbers, "Precious robbers please take this also. I know that we people from Lhathok are always traveling and you might need a cup on the road." So he gave it to them, even though they had over-looked it at first.

The point here is that we usually think we own the things we have. It is true that they are our possessions but eventually they go here and there. Things are passed around, so clinging to our pos-sessions does not make sense. If we place too much importance on possessions and people want to rob us, we could fight them and in the process lose not only our possessions but also our very life.

We should know what has a greater value. We should not risk our lives for something, such as the various things we have accumulated, that is not as significant as life itself. Possessions are only relatively important. The point here is that, even if we lose our possessions, we should not be too affected by it and dedicate them to the people who have taken them away. This is the practice of a bodhisattva.

13

> Even if another were to cut off our head
> Though we had not the slightest fault,
> To take on their negativity
> With compassion is the practice of a bodhisattva.

This is extremely difficult to do, so let us leave this practice to very highly realized beings. There is no need to explain it.

14

> Although someone broadcasts throughout a billion worlds
> A legion of unpleasant things about us,
> In return, with a mind full of love,
> To tell of their qualities is the practice of a bodhisattva.

This is also difficult. Being insulted and slandered throughout a billion worlds would probably be too hard for us to handle. Even when someone right in front of us says bad things about us, our expression changes and our face turns red. Yet, if a person were to say something bad about us while they were not in our presence, we would not hear it and therefore not be bothered by these words. So it is best not to listen to insults. If we cannot avoid it and someone puts us down right to our face, it is better to turn our attention elsewhere and not heed what they say. If we pay attention to them, we could become angry, and once anger arises it is very difficult to subdue. Therefore, the best thing for beginners is to avoid listening to negative talk about themselves. If we do hear something unpleasant, we can ignore it and concentrate on something else.

15

Before a large crowd, if someone were to speak harsh
  words
And expose our hidden faults,
To see this person as a spiritual friend
And bow with respect is the practice of a bodhisattva.

If a person is straightforward and says something true that we do not like to hear, we could become quite upset. Later, however, when we think it over and look honestly at our mind, we realize that he or she was actually right and we did make a mistake. When that happens, we can revise our stance and shift our way of thinking. We do not necessarily take that person as a teacher, but we can learn from him or her and find some useful instruction in what was said.

16

If another whom we cherished as our child
Came to see us as an enemy,
Like a mother whose child is gravely ill,
To love this person even more is the practice of a
  bodhisattva.

It is very difficult when someone we have trusted completely turns on us. It is one of the most painful things that can happen to anyone. However, as we discussed earlier, it is always possible that hidden, in even the people closest to us are secrets or feelings that we do not know about. There may be some reason the person changed, some justification for their action. We do not know, but we should seek an explanation, because people have their own reasons for acting as they do.

17

> If people who are our equal or less
> Through pride would put us down,
> With respect as for a teacher
> To place them above us is the practice of a bodhisattva.

This is not to say that we have to bear any insult like a cow. No matter how much they are put down, cows cannot reply or do anything else, so they do not react. We do not have to be passive like that. What this stanza means is that when someone insults us, we should not react with anger. If we are overpowered by our negative emotions, we become unbalanced and lose control, and this should not happen. It is better to be stable and centered within ourselves so that we can respond in a good way, based on who we actually are. Some people with a mild nature have a way of saying "I'm sorry" that is nicely done, and other people have a more direct way of talking. Whatever our character may be, we do not have to keep on enduring insults and doing nothing at all. We can respond to an insult without losing our balance or letting negative emotions take over.

Of course, we have to respect others, but before we show someone the same respect that we would give to a teacher, we should respect ourselves. If we do not regard ourselves as worthwhile, if we put ourselves down, we will not be able to value and respect others. Therefore, we begin by showing respect to ourselves, and then we will be able to do the same for others.

18

> Though stricken with poverty and always scorned,
> Plagued by grave illness and bad spirits too,
> Not to lose heart but take on the misdeeds
> And misery of all beings is the practice of a bodhisattva.

This stanza is about not getting discouraged even if we are very poor and have no possessions; even if people scorn us and we are sick; and even if terrible things happen to us all at once. We can relate to these situations by knowing that Dharma practitioners need experiences, even when they are all negative, because they give us knowledge. Through experience we learn what to do and not to do, as well as what behavior needs improvement for the next time. Planning for our future is filtered through the experience we have gained.

Whatever our negative situation may be, we need to take a long-term view and sustain our hope with an aspiration, which could be a goal that we seek or a way that we want to be. Our aspiration is like a spy keeping an eye out for opportunities. In the olden days, a spy would sit on a high mountain and survey everything that was happening. Looking down the road into the future and maintaining our hope is like that watcher. When an opportunity arises that fits our plan, we can call on our experience to take advantage of it. When experience and hope join together, whatever difficult, negative, or tragic situations occur in our life, we can always pull ourselves together and start anew.

19

> Although famous with crowds bowing down
> And affluent as a god of wealth,
> To see samsara's riches as devoid of essence
> And remain free of arrogance is the practice of a
> bodhisattva.

Sometimes we can become arrogant, so here is an example of what we could do about it. Suppose there is a big ocean that has a whole variety of things in it and a small child is playing at the edge of the water. One day the child finds some colorful pebbles. Another day it finds different kinds of shells. On still another day it comes upon some precious stones. Whatever the child finds makes it happy—pebble, shell, or gem. It is very excited about all its discoveries, but nonetheless the child does not think that it has found all the riches in the whole ocean.

This is a good way to be, for even though we may have and know a lot, we should not think, "I have everything." "I know everything." Obviously, this is not the case. If we know something and become too proud of it, we become arrogant and that always closes doors and blocks opportunities. Furthermore, even when we know something and we know that we know it, we will find that when we discuss it with others, they might have another opinion. They might have an unusual way of describing something or a different way of presenting it, and we can learn from these differences. We will have a new experience and expand our understanding.

Although the text says that we should not be arrogant, that does not mean that we have to be timid. If we do not know, we can say that we do not know and do so with a sense of confidence.

CHAPTER 14

Taming Our Mind

20

Not conquering the foe of our anger
Yet fighting with enemies outside, we'll just make more.
Therefore, with an army of love and compassion
To tame our mind is the practice of a bodhisattva.

OUR ANGER IS OUR ACTUAL ENEMY. It is an obstacle that cuts us off from the cause of higher states of rebirth and the definitive excellence that is liberation. If we do not tame it, then outer enemies will simply multiply. They will increase to the same extent that we try to overpower them. And they could present a danger to our lives and to our ability to keep any of the three sets of vows (individual liberation, bodhisattva, and tantric) we may have taken.

Since we are the ones who make one another into enemies, they can proliferate without limit. By creating such projections, we are engaging in actions that are detrimental. Why is this so? Because there is not one living being who has not been our mother or father, and therefore they should all be the objects of our compassion. On the other hand, there is not one living being who has not been our enemy. In this way, all living beings are equally our friends and enemies, so being attached to some and feeling hatred for others makes no sense. Through a mind that sees this equality, we should tame the enemy of our own anger with an army of great compassion. This is the practice of a true bodhisattva.

21

> Desired objects are like water mixed with salt:
> To the extent we enjoy them craving increases.
> To give up instantly everything
> That arouses attachment is the practice of a bodhisattva.

Pleasurable objects are usually listed as falling into five different categories: attractive forms, pleasant sounds, fragrant smells, delicious tastes, and pleasing objects of touch. Like salty water, they cannot satisfy our desires. To the extent that we enjoy these objects, to that same extent will we be tormented by our desiring. Not only are we not satisfied, but our desires increase. For example, if someone suffering from thirst drinks salt water, their thirst will not be quenched and, further, they will want to drink even more. This is how craving expands.

The verse continues: "to give up instantly everything that arouses attachment...." Giving up attachment to our enjoyment of pleasurable objects can be illustrated with the following example. As we move through our daily lives, we experience a variety of objects that engage our senses. When we are focused on one of these and feel attachment to it, we should quickly abandon it. Why so? Because eliminating any object that causes afflictions to appear is an effective way of suppressing these negative emotions. In my own experience, for example, when I receive something that I like very much, I immediately try to pass it on to someone else. Holding on to things we strongly desire will just cause problems.

22

Things as they appear are our own mind;
The mind itself is forever free of fabrications.
Knowing this, not to engage the attributes
Of a subject or object is the practice of a bodhisattva.

If, with valid reasoning, we were to look for an inherent nature in the whole range of phenomena that appear as objects for our sensory experience, we would not find a single one that has its own essence. This is because these objects are all imputed by our conceptual mind, or, following the first line of the verse, we could say these objects are just an appearance of our mind. And the mind itself, the true nature of mind, is "forever free of fabrications." Analyzing with reasonings found in the Abhidharma or the Mahayana, we will find that no phenomenon can be established as having an essence through any kind of mental construct or fabrication. These are often summarized into what are called "the four extremes": arising from itself, arising from something other, arising from a combination of the two, or arising from neither.

By engaging in such an analysis, we can look into how we grasp on to the attributes, or characteristics, of a subject and an object. Over time, we will come to see that the outer apprehended object and the inner apprehending mind are the result of habitual patterns that cling to phenomena as real. If we can bring to an end the mental activity, or conceptualizing, that results from these habitual patterns, we can rest in meditative concentration with a one-pointed focus on reality itself. This is the profound practice of a bodhisattva.

23

> When encountering a pleasing object,
> See it as a rainbow in summer—
> A beautiful appearance, but not real—
> To give up attachment is the practice of a bodhisattva.

When a beautiful and pleasing form is experienced by ordinary individuals, it appears differently to each one. Further, what is pleasing and what is not pleasing arise in connection with one another: it is not possible for them to arise separately. When a desired object appears along with its characteristics and habitual patterns, the danger arises that in becoming attached to it, we will create a state of mind convinced of something that is not true: we think that the object is real. To curb this tendency, we should realize that just like a rainbow in summer, these appearing objects have no essence.

When we speak of a summer rainbow, almost anyone will know that it is like an illusion and not truly existent. As we have seen in looking at dependent arising, when something pleasant appears to our mind, what is unpleasant is not far away. However, it is especially the case that when something attractive starts to appear, we direct powerful thoughts toward it and take an illusory phenomenon to be real. Therefore, bodhisattvas practice giving up attachment.

24

> All suffering is like our child dying in a dream;
> To take these delusive appearances as real, how
>   exhausting!
> Therefore, when dealing with difficult situations,
> To see them as delusions is the practice of a bodhisattva.

There are times we are so completely absorbed in a pleasant object that if something unpleasant comes along, we do not experience that unpleasantness or any negative feeling. More commonly, however, due to our habitual patterns, anger and other negative emotions do arise, and then we need to rely on a variety of antidotes. By the mere fact of being alive, we will experience suffering, such as not getting what we want and getting what we do not want. When we meet up with suffering, we need to orient ourselves in a direct and useful way. In brief, when suffering arises, this is as illusory as a beloved child dying in a dream. From time immemorial, habitual patterns that take things to be real have surfaced in our mind, and these confused appearances are arising without a break. Since all the appearances we meet are like this, the potential for suffering is unlimited.

It is this clinging to things that creates an ongoing current of suffering, which, however, is not necessary. It arises due to the fact that although we perceive separate appearances, these perceptions happen so swiftly that they seem to be flowing together in a single stream, and this we take to be truly existent. However, if we turn and look from the perspective of the appearance itself, we can see that it is not truly established; it is neither stable nor enduring. Therefore, when our mind reaches out and grasps things as real, we are the ones who are creating the conditions for our own suffering. For all these good reasons, to see all appearances as illusion-like, not taking them to be real, is the practice of a bodhisattva.

CHAPTER 15

The Six Perfections

25

If those aspiring to enlightenment give even their body
    away,
What need is there to mention outer objects?
Therefore, without hope of return or a good result,
To be generous is the practice of a bodhisattva.

THE NEXT STANZAS DESCRIBE the six perfections, or the six paramitas, the first of which is generosity. Many religions and spiritual paths agree on the importance of giving, because we can all see that this benefits others directly. For Buddhism, in particular, being generous is important because it directly counteracts our attachments.

When we help others, we should do so with an intelligence that is able to analyze the situation. True generosity requires some wisdom—a clear understanding of ourselves who are giving, what we are giving, and to whom we are giving. If we give using our intelligence, then generosity benefits both ourselves and others. We should not give just for the sake of giving or from an old habit. Further, in the process of giving, we should not become distracted, for losing our focus diminishes the scope and effect of our activity. When we are generous and wise, our giving benefits others and also helps us to deepen our practice as we move along the path.

26

If lacking discipline, we can't even help ourselves,
Wishing to benefit others is just a joke.
Therefore, to maintain a discipline
Free of desire for samsara is the practice of a bodhisattva.

When misunderstood, the perfections can have a darker side, which is metaphorically called a "demon." The downside of the perfection of discipline is called "the demon of austerity"— taking on discipline as a hardship and making it into a struggle. Done right, discipline is taken on joyfully and with a clear understanding of why engaging in it is good. For example, many people nowadays have given up eating meat. Why would we do that? We should not become vegetarian just because someone says we should, or because the Buddha taught that we should not eat meat, or because it is the custom where we live, or because giving up meat would give us a good reputation. If we give up eating meat for these reasons, it might be better not to do it at all, because our decision is not sincerely motivated.

In the beginning, we have a certain feeling about not eating meat. Then we can ask ourselves questions, such as what are the real benefits? After careful consideration, we become certain that this is the right thing to do. Our answer has to come from within, inspired by real conviction, so that when we do give up eating meat, it does not become a hardship or a struggle but something we do with joy and intelligence. It is the same with any discipline in the Vinaya, the Mahayana, or the Vajrayana. Whatever we give up or whatever we do, we should first feel a connection to the practice and then be very clear why we are doing this and not something else. When we act this way, our discipline becomes very inspiring.

27

> For bodhisattvas aspiring to a wealth of virtue,
> Anything that harms is a treasury of jewels.
> Therefore, never turning aggressive or angry,
> To be patient is the practice of a bodhisattva.

The third perfection is patience, which also has an obstacle, called "the demon of too much struggling" or "too much forbearance." Patience, like generosity and discipline, should not be too extreme, but should arise freely through our understanding. When we have love and compassion, we naturally understand why the afflictions occur and do not struggle to be patient.

For example, when sick, some people keep on struggling with the illness and refuse to take any treatment. That is excessive forbearance. In general, we should not put up with everything or do everything that anyone asks us to do. Enduring too much has the drawback of giving others the opportunity to do negative things. We could also be too patient with our own afflictions. Excessive forbearance is also a problem because we must clearly know the reasons for what we are doing and not just blindly continue without reflection, especially if it concerns something we find objectionable. Otherwise, if without reason a person told us to eat something obnoxious, we would do it without thinking. It might not be easy fo us, but we can immediately say, "I will not do that." This is not a problem but the proper way of practicing patience. It must be a response that comes from deep within.

28

> If Hearers and Solitary Realizers for their benefit alone
> Practice diligence as if their heads were on fire,
> To develop diligence, the wellspring of all qualities
> That benefit every being, is the practice of a bodhisattva.

The demon of diligence is struggling or pushing too hard. This is a problem, for true diligence means taking joy in doing positive things. Whatever practices we do should be done in a spontaneous and natural way. Essentially, meditation practice is about entering into the nature of suchness. It is not about beating ourselves up and forcing ourselves to do something. There is no need to strain and think, "I don't want to do this, but I have to." It should be a natural reaction, as if a fire were burning on our head. (This example in the verse refers to practitioners from the Foundational Vehicle, who are thought to have the more limited aim of freeing only themselves from samsara.) If our hair catches fire, we do not say, "I should probably get rid of this fire, but I don't want to." Nor do we turn it over in our minds, consult our teachers, conduct research, or send off a stream of letters. Without thinking, we immediately jump up and extinguish the fire effortlessly. True diligence happens with a lively interest and joyful spontaneity. We do something because we see clearly that it is important and essential.

A while ago, the BBC broadcast a program about birth, old age, sickness, and death. Watching it, I saw many people who were suffering and thought how much they could be helped by Dharma if they really understood it. When I see millions of people suffering, I feel completely energized to do something about it. It is not a struggle or a matter of coercing myself to do something I don't want to. Diligence is really about our motivation: we feel totally absorbed and joyful in wanting to do something.

There is a lot to say, but time flies by. It is like the poet who was inspired and writing furiously. He had to break for lunch, but he was so immersed in his poetry that he continued to write while eating his bread. Later he discovered that he had been dunking his bread in the ink.

29

Knowing that deep insight fully endowed with calm
abiding
Completely conquers all afflictions,
To cultivate a concentration that transcends
The four formless states is the practice of a bodhisattva.

Meditation, the fifth perfection, has a demon called "attachment to experience." It is not easy to fully understand meditative experience. The verse refers to formless states of meditation, which are categorized as follows: limitless space, limitless consciousness, nothing whatsoever, and neither existence nor nonexistence. Much has been written about these, but they lie outside the main point here. What we need to know is that when we meditate, all sorts of experiences will come, both good and not so good. These experiences, however, are not important. Here, the key is the extent to which our meditation serves as an antidote to our afflictions. How many obscurations and how many afflictions have been subdued or cleared away? This is the true test of meditation, not what wonderful or special experiences we might have. In fact, if we become attached to these experiences, that is a problem.

30

Without wisdom the five perfections
Cannot bring forth full awakening.
To cultivate wisdom endowed with skillful means
And free of concepts in the three domains is the practice of
a bodhisattva.

Wisdom is the sixth perfection and its demon is the obstacle called "the demon of increasing poison." This obstacle is very serious, even monstrous, like an immense beast with nine heads. It comes up after studying, reflecting, and analyzing, when we reach a certain conceptual understanding and our afflictions are not too active. We find something our conceptualizing mind can seize upon and take pride in. One way our mind does this is through "concepts in the three domains," which relate to the three aspects of any activity: a subject, an object, and an action. When our mind conceptualizes like this in a very solid and concrete manner, our view becomes extreme. We are convinced that we have found the "right" way and we are proud of it. This process resembles how the rigid views of people caught in the mundane world are developed. Nowadays, these stubborn positions are a great problem. And they also contradict progress as it is understood in the Dharma: As we move along the path, inferior views are gradually surpassed by superior ones, until finally there is no view at all, nothing to be seized upon. Therefore, we should not go to an extreme and cling to one position as the truth. Our view of how things are is not something to grasp with a tight fist.

We might think, "I'm a Buddhist, and my Buddhism is the best. I can look down on others." When our intelligence takes this form, instead of reducing aversion and attachment, it increases them. We should not relate to others in such a way that we put them down and raise ourselves up; rather, we focus on developing our wisdom through listening, reflecting, and meditating. If it causes our afflictions to increase, wisdom turns into a demon. When our view or practice harms others, they run contrary to Buddhist teachings, for their very basis is to cherish all living beings in our heart. Developing wisdom through listening, reflecting, and meditating is central to Buddhism, but more important are living beings.

CHAPTER 16
Avoiding Pitfalls

31

> Not examining our confusion, we could masquerade
> As a practitioner while not in harmony with the Dharma.
> Therefore, to continually examine our confusion
> And discard it is the practice of a bodhisattva.

THIS STANZA ADDRESSES those of us who call ourselves Dharma practitioners. What is the definition of practice? Taming our mind. Those of us who are supposed to be practicing Dharma should carefully examine ourselves—our body, speech, and mind—and become mindful of what we are doing. Otherwise, it is quite possible that although we have the form of a practitioner, we are not really practicing Dharma.

Watching carefully to find our own faults, however, does not mean that we have to look down on ourselves or feel that we are worse than others. We do not have to throw ourselves into the river. This is too extreme. What it does mean is that practicing the Dharma is like learning how to dance. When we are learning how to move our arms and legs, we can practice in a room full of mirrors. Seeing our reflection directly, we observe how we are doing even before someone else tells us what is wrong. We all have faults—that is natural and not surprising. We also know how to improve, because we know, or can learn, what to correct and change. Further, we realize that what we are doing is for our own benefit. So if we find some faults or mistakes that we need to change, there is nothing wrong with us; these are just what we need to work on. This is what is meant by "taming our mind."

Then we might ask, "How do I examine my confusion?" Among the many different ways of investigating, there is one we do all the time: We are always on the lookout for the faults of others—what problems they have or what is wrong with what they do or think. Our mind is turned outward to judge others and not inward to see what we ourselves are doing wrong or what problems we might have. In this case, everything is reversed. For the wrong reasons, we think others are more important, and further, we do not consider ourselves to be the center of concern when we should. We should be looking inward at ourselves to see what to give up and what to change. If we do not try to do this, improving ourselves will be a distant dream.

Most important is to be mindful of what transpires within us. For example, when we do not want anything bad to happen to us, we are very cautious in what we do. We are careful to avoid even a pinprick. In the same way, when we are working with our mind, we should be alert and conscientious, examining carefully what we are doing. Gradually, we will come to understand how we are and who we are, and with this knowledge as a basis, we can look within and see what is confused or mistaken and what is not.

One simple way to examine ourselves is to look at photographs or videos that show how we talk and behave. Sometimes, before watching a video of myself speaking, I would feel that I had said something really significant. But later, when I actually saw the film, I was a little ashamed, because what it showed was not exactly what I had imagined. When we watch ourselves like this, we can find the things that need improvement. In sum, whether we are looking inward at our mind or outward at a reflection, we should observe ourselves with clear attention.

32

> If afflictions compel us to fault other bodhisattvas,
> We ourselves will be diminished.
> Therefore, not to mention the faults of those
> Who have entered the Mahayana path is the practice of a
> bodhisattva.

This instruction is not limited to bodhisattvas. We should not say bad things about anyone, whether or not they are bodhisattvas. It is not the same thing, however, if we know that pointing out someone's mistakes will help them to change. Generally speaking, since it is not easy to change another person, we should avoid criticism. Other people do not like to hear it and, further, laying out their faults will create problems and troubles for us. We who are supposed to be practicing the Dharma should be trying to do whatever brings happiness to ourselves and others. Since faultfinding does not bring any benefit, we should carefully avoid it.

In my own case, people tell me negative things about others and describe numerous faults. In a way, this is normal and not surprising. However, enumerating faults is not an effective way to bring about change. Even if we point out someone's faults all the time, it will rarely alter the person or make anything better. If we really want to help someone, perhaps we can say something once in a pleasant way so that the person can readily understand, "Oh yes, this is something I need to change." However, it is better not to repeat our comments, because if we keep mentioning faults, not only will it not truly help, it will disturb others to no good effect. Therefore not mentioning the faults of others is the practice of bodhisattvas.

33

Disputes arise from wanting honor and gain;
The activities of listening, reflecting, and meditating
    decline.
Therefore, to give up attachment to the homes
Of friends, relatives, and donors is the practice of a
    bodhisattva.

All we really need to do for practice is to study, reflect, and meditate. However, these days it is common in the East and West that desire for honor and gain creates problems. Imitation monks, phony lamas, fake tulkus, and false gods turn up, and because of this, it is difficult to find the right kind of study, reflection, and meditation. It is very important for everyone to be careful about this and try to see clearly what is genuine and what is false. If someone says, "I am a lama," or "I am a tulku," or "I am a god," we do not have to immediately follow them. First, investigate to see whether they are genuine or not and whether we should make a connection with them. It is important to use our critical faculties along with giving up attachments.

34

Harsh words trouble the minds of others
And diminish a bodhisattva's conduct.
Therefore, to give up rough words
Not pleasing to others is the practice of a bodhisattva.

This instruction is similar to what was said in stanza 32. Sometimes harsh words must be said in order to help someone, but generally when we speak harshly, it is because we are angry, and it does not help. It is difficult to speak harsh words with love and compassion. In these situations, we can take ourselves as an example. Putting ourselves in someone else's place, we ask, "If someone said these words to me in that way, how would I feel?" When we truly think of others, we will find some part of them that resembles us, because every one of us experiences pleasure and pain. Before we act or speak, thinking of others as similar to us is quite useful.

35

> Once they've become a habit, afflictions resist their
> remedies.
> Alert attention, the noble being, seizes the weapon of an
> antidote
> And slays in a flash its enemy, every affliction—
> Excessive desire and all the others; such is the practice of a
> bodhisattva.

In general, we may find it easy to read these verses, but not so easy to follow their instructions. Cutting through afflictions is difficult, especially once they have come up, because we are so habituated to them. What we can do is recognize that anger is about to arise and then take action. We can use a method or remedy that will deter the anger from becoming a full-blown negative emotion.

One way I have found effective is to recall a particular lama whom I trust and like and whose speech is pleasing. For example, one lama may have taught me why anger or aversion undermines practice and how negative its effects are, so I bring to mind that lama's advice: "Don't be influenced by the afflictions. Be careful!"

Whenever I sense that anger is about to arise, I just remember that lama and his instructions. When I do this, it helps me not to be overpowered by the negative emotion. My closeness to that lama and my respect for him makes me think, "This is not right. It goes against my lama's words." Another way of using this method is to remember a book we really like that deals with the afflictions, and bring these passages to mind. Then, like a sound becoming ever louder, when we sense that an affliction is on the rise, we can turn the volume back down before it fully manifests. This, too, can be useful.

CHAPTER 17

Key Points
and Dedication

36

In brief, wherever we are and whatever we do,
While staying continually mindful and alert
To the state of our mind,
To benefit others is the practice of a bodhisattva.

W HEN WE TALK about examining our actions, it does not
mean that we have to examine ourselves nonstop,
twenty-four hours a day. We could lighten up. For example, when we watch very long movies or work on a computer,
we are told not to look at the screen continuously. After a while,
it will help our eyes if we get up and look around a little bit, to
gaze at the greenery, for example. We give our eyes a break. Sim-
ilarly, although we should thoroughly examine our mind, after
a while, we may need to take a break, otherwise we become too
tired. To look after ourselves means that we should care for ourselves. Just as we look after our body, we should also look after
our mind. Our mind is key and usually we are quite fond of it,
so we should take good care of it.

We are advised to benefit others, and we may want to do something for them, but that could be difficult if we do not know what to do. It may even seem that there is nothing we can do. As we move around in our lives, people appear isolated, sitting in their own space, or maybe they seem too solemn. We just want to give them something sweet or helpful, but that does not seem to be the appropriate thing to do. So there are times when we feel frustrated, because there is no way we can help that feels right. When this happens, what we can do is just a small action right where we are, such as picking up a little garbage and putting it in the place where it belongs. Even if we do that and nothing else, we can say, "I've done something good." It is not a big deal, but it is a start.

This is exactly how we should accumulate merit. We cannot do something great all at once. We may want to, but it is quite difficult. This is why it is said that we accumulate merit ounce by ounce—just like that, little by little. We accomplish something small that makes our mind happy and then we feel that we could do a little more. In this way, the small, positive things we do will accumulate over time.

37

To dispel the suffering of limitless beings
With a wisdom not tainted by concepts of the three
    domains,
To dedicate for full awakening all merit
Gained by this effort is the practice of a bodhisattva.

This dedication is the last of the thirty-seven practices of a bodhisattva. It is an excellent one, too, for it gathers all the merit accumulated from these practices and dedicates it to all living beings throughout space that they may attain happiness and be free of suffering.

c

> Following the meaning of the sutras and treatises
> And the teachings of genuine masters too,
> I have given these thirty-seven verses of a bodhisattva's
>   practice
> For the benefit of those who would train on this path.

These thirty-seven verses interweave the key points of practice with explanations of their meaning. They are given for those on the bodhisattva path to practice and blend with their experience. The text is based on several sources that provide the basis for a bodhisattva's training: practices found in the sutras of the Hinayana and Mahayana taught by our guide, the perfect Buddha; the four tantras of the Vajrayana; and all the treatises that elucidate the systems of thought in these texts. Also connected to the practice of a bodhisattva are the oral instructions of the previous genuine masters and the advice of spiritual friends. All of these were put into thirty-seven verses for the sake of those fortunate ones who wish to study and engage in the training of a bodhisattva.

d

> Since my intelligence is limited and little trained,
> The artistry of this text will not please the learned.
> Yet relying on the sutras and teachings of genuine masters,
> These practices, I trust, are free of confusion.

The author Thogme Zangpo claims that his wisdom is inferior and that his practice has produced only a few positive qualities. Since these verses are not like the major treatises from India and Tibet based on reasonings, this text has none of the perfect artistry that weaves together words with their meaning and pleases the experts. Nevertheless, the meaning of the verses and the stages of practice are presented just as they are in the sutras, tantras, and treatises. The explanations are given following the writings and oral instructions transmitted from the Buddha down to Thogme Zangpo's own root lama; he has not added anything of his own. Therefore, he trusts that these practices of a bodhisattva are trustworthy and free of confusion.

> For an inferior intellect like mine it is difficult
> To measure the vast activity of a bodhisattva,
> So I pray that genuine masters will tolerate
> All the defects here, the contradictions, non sequiturs, and
> so forth.

The vast activity of a bodhisattva is so profound that it is difficult to fathom, and so it belongs to the realm experienced by advanced bodhisattvas. For those of us with inferior intellects, such as the author claims to have, it is quite impossible to measure. Alleging that he is not an expert, Thogme Zangpo notes that defects could appear in his writing, such as contradictions or a lack of coherence between what was said earlier and later. Recognizing these faults, he confesses his mistakes in the presence of bodhisattvas and those with the wisdom eye of Dharma, supplicating them to have patience with him.

> By the virtue arising from these verses,
> Through ultimate and relative bodhichitta,
> May all beings become equal to the Protector Chenrezik,
> Who dwells in neither extreme of existence or peace.

With this verse, the bodhisattva Ngülchu Thogme Zangpo brings to a close his treatise on the practices of a bodhisattva, presented in thirty-seven verses that are easy to understand. All the utterly pure virtue, whether great or small, that has arisen from composing this text he dedicates so that all living beings, equal to the extent of space, through the power of great compassion do not remain in the extreme of peace, and through the power of great wisdom do not remain in the extreme of existence. He prays that freed in this way from the delusions of nirvana and samsara, all living beings become equal to Chenrezik, who resides in neither of these two extremes. With this all-embracing aspiration, Thogme Zangpo concludes his text on the practices of a bodhisattva.

The Thirty-Seven Practices of a Bodhisattva

by Ngülchu Thogme Zangpo

a   Namo Lokeshvaraya.
Seeing that all phenomena neither come nor go
Yet seeking only to benefit living beings,
The supreme master and the Protector Chenrezik
I honor continually with body, speech, and mind.

b   Perfect buddhas, source of all benefit and happiness,
Arise through accomplishing the genuine Dharma;
Since this in turn depends on knowing how to practice,
The practices of a bodhisattva will be explained.

1   Now that we have a vessel of leisure and resources, so difficult
        to find,
So that we may bring ourselves and others across the ocean
        of samsara,
Without a break during day or night
To listen, reflect, and meditate is the practice of a bodhisattva.

2   Attachment to friends churns like water;
    Aversion to enemies burns like fire.
    Dark with ignorance—not knowing what to adopt or reject—
    To give up this homeland is the practice of a bodhisattva.

3   By leaving harmful places, afflictions gradually decline.
    With no distractions, virtuous activity naturally grows.
    With a clear mind, certainty in the Dharma arises.
    To rely on solitude is the practice of a bodhisattva.

4   Everyone will part from relatives and old friends;
    The wealth of long labor will be left behind;
    The guest, consciousness, leaves its lodging, the body, behind:
    To give up concern for this life is the practice of a bodhisattva.

5   Make friends with these and the three poisons grow;
    The activities of listening, reflecting, and meditating decline
    While love and compassion are destroyed.
    To cast off bad friends is the practice of a bodhisattva.

6   Rely on this one and defects disappear;
    Qualities increase like the waxing moon.
    To cherish a genuine spiritual friend
    More than our own body is the practice of a bodhisattva.

7   Captive themselves in the prison of samsara,
    Whom could the worldly gods protect?
    Therefore, when seeking protection, to go for refuge
    To the unfailing Three Jewels is the practice of a bodhisattva.

8   The sufferings of the lower realms so difficult to bear
      Come from misdeeds, thus the Buddha taught.
      Therefore, even at the risk of our life,
      Never to commit these actions is the practice of a bodhisattva.

9   Happiness in the three realms is like dew on a
                blade of grass—
      Its nature is to evaporate in an instant.
      To strive for the supreme state of liberation
      That never changes is the practice of a bodhisattva.

10   From time beyond time, our mothers have cared for us;
      If they suffer, what good is our own happiness?
      Thus, to liberate living beings beyond number,
      To engender bodhichitta is the practice of a bodhisattva.

11   All suffering comes from wanting happiness for ourselves;
      Perfect buddhas arise from the intention to benefit others.
      Therefore, to truly exchange our happiness
      For the suffering of others is the practice of a bodhisattva.

12   If out of great desire someone steals all our wealth
      Or makes another do so,
      To dedicate our body, possessions, and all merit of the
                three times
      To this person is the practice of a bodhisattva.

13   Even if another were to cut off our head
      Though we had not the slightest fault,
      To take on their negativity
      With compassion is the practice of a bodhisattva.

14 Although someone broadcasts throughout a billion worlds
    A legion of unpleasant things about us,
    In return, with a mind full of love,
    To tell of their qualities is the practice of a bodhisattva.

15 Before a large crowd, if someone were to speak harsh words
    And expose our hidden faults,
    To see this person as a spiritual friend
    And bow with respect is the practice of a bodhisattva.

16 If another whom we cherished as our child
    Came to see us as an enemy,
    Like a mother whose child is gravely ill,
    To love this person even more is the practice of a bodhisattva.

17 If people who are our equal or less
    Through pride would put us down,
    With respect as for a teacher
    To place them above us is the practice of a bodhisattva.

18 Though stricken with poverty and always scorned,
    Plagued by grave illness and bad spirits too,
    Not to lose heart but take on the misdeeds
    And misery of all beings is the practice of a bodhisattva.

19 Although famous with crowds bowing down
    And affluent as a god of wealth,
    To see samsara's riches as devoid of essence
    And remain free of arrogance is the practice of a bodhisattva.

20   Not conquering the foe of our anger
     Yet fighting with enemies outside, we'll just make more.
     Therefore, with an army of love and compassion
     To tame our mind is the practice of a bodhisattva.

21   Desired objects are like water mixed with salt:
     To the extent we enjoy them craving increases.
     To give up instantly everything
     That arouses attachment is the practice of a bodhisattva.

22   Things as they appear are our own mind;
     The mind itself is forever free of fabrications.
     Knowing this, not to engage the attributes
     Of a subject or object is the practice of a bodhisattva.

23   When encountering a pleasing object,
     See it as a rainbow in summer—
     A beautiful appearance, but not real—
     To give up attachment is the practice of a bodhisattva.

24   All suffering is like our child dying in a dream;
     To take these delusive appearances as real, how exhausting!
     Therefore, when dealing with difficult situations,
     To see them as delusions is the practice of a bodhisattva.

25   If those aspiring to enlightenment give even their body away,
     What need is there to mention outer objects?
     Therefore, without hope of return or a good result,
     To be generous is the practice of a bodhisattva.

26   If lacking discipline, we can't even help ourselves,
     Wishing to benefit others is just a joke.
     Therefore, to maintain a discipline
     Free of desire for samsara is the practice of a bodhisattva.

27   For bodhisattvas aspiring to a wealth of virtue,
     Anything that harms is a treasury of jewels.
     Therefore, never turning aggressive or angry,
     To be patient is the practice of a bodhisattva.

28   If Hearers and Solitary Realizers for their benefit alone
     Practice diligence as if their heads were on fire,
     To develop diligence, the wellspring of all qualities
     That benefit every being, is the practice of a bodhisattva.

29   Knowing that deep insight fully endowed with calm abiding
     Completely conquers all afflictions,
     To cultivate a concentration that transcends
     The four formless states is the practice of a bodhisattva.

30   Without wisdom the five perfections
     Cannot bring forth full awakening.
     To cultivate wisdom endowed with skillful means
     And free of concepts in the three domains is the practice of a
       bodhisattva.

31   Not examining our confusion, we could masquerade
     As a practitioner while not in harmony with the Dharma.
     Therefore, to continually examine our confusion
     And discard it is the practice of a bodhisattva.

32   If afflictions compel us to fault other bodhisattvas,
      We ourselves will be diminished.
      Therefore, not to mention the faults of those
      Who have entered the Mahayana path is the practice of a
         bodhisattva.

33   Disputes arise from wanting honor and gain;
      The activities of listening, reflecting, and meditating decline.
      Therefore, to give up attachment to the homes
      Of friends, relatives, and donors is the practice of a
         bodhisattva.

34   Harsh words trouble the minds of others
      And diminish a bodhisattva's conduct.
      Therefore, to give up rough words
      Not pleasing to others is the practice of a bodhisattva.

35   Once they've become a habit, afflictions resist their remedies.
      Alert attention, the noble being, seizes the weapon of an
         antidote
      And slays in a flash its enemy, every affliction—
      Excessive desire and all the others; such is the practice of a
         bodhisattva.

36   In brief, wherever we are and whatever we do,
      While staying continually mindful and alert
      To the state of our mind,
      To benefit others is the practice of a bodhisattva.

37   To dispel the suffering of limitless beings
      With a wisdom not tainted by concepts of the three domains,
      To dedicate for full awakening all merit
      Gained by this effort is the practice of a bodhisattva.

c   Following the meaning of the sutras and treatises
And the teachings of genuine masters too,
I have given these thirty-seven verses of a bodhisattva's
    practice
For the benefit of those who would train on this path.

d   Since my intelligence is limited and little trained,
The artistry of this text will not please the learned.
Yet relying on the sutras and teachings of genuine masters,
These practices, I trust, are free of confusion.

e   For an inferior intellect like mine it is difficult
To measure the vast activity of a bodhisattva,
So I pray that genuine masters will tolerate
All the defects here, the contradictions, non sequiturs, and
    so forth.

f   By the virtue arising from these verses,
Through ultimate and relative bodhichitta,
May all beings become equal to the Protector Chenrezik,
Who dwells in neither extreme of existence or peace.

For the benefit of self and other, the monk Thogme, a proponent of scriptures and reasoning, composed these verses at Ngülchu Rinchen Cave.

༄༅། །རྒྱལ་བའི་སྲས་ཀྱི་ལག་ལེན་སུམ་ཅུ་སོ་བདུན་མ་བཞུགས་སོ། །

༄༅། །ན་མོ་ལོ་ཀེ་ཤྭ་རཱ་ཡ།
གང་གིས་ཆོས་ཀུན་འགྲོ་འོང་མེད་གཟིགས་ཀྱང་། །
འགྲོ་བའི་དོན་ལ་གཅིག་ཏུ་བརྩོན་མཛད་པའི། །
བླ་མ་མཆོག་དང་སྤྱན་རས་གཟིགས་མགོན་ལ། །
རྟག་ཏུ་སྒོ་གསུམ་གུས་པས་ཕྱག་འཚལ་ལོ། །

ཕན་བདེའི་འབྱུང་གནས་རྫོགས་པའི་སངས་རྒྱས་རྣམས། །
དམ་ཆོས་བསྒྲུབས་ལས་བྱུང་སྟེ་དེ་ཡང་ནི། །
དེ་ཡི་ལག་ལེན་ཤེས་ལ་རག་ལས་པས། །
རྒྱལ་སྲས་རྣམས་ཀྱི་ལག་ལེན་བཤད་པར་བྱ། །

དལ་འབྱོར་གྲུ་ཆེན་རྙེད་དཀའ་ཐོབ་དུས་འདིར། །
བདག་གཞན་འཁོར་བའི་མཚོ་ལས་བསྒྲལ་བྱའི་ཕྱིར། །
ཉིན་དང་མཚན་དུ་གཡེལ་བ་མེད་པར་ནི། །
ཉན་སེམས་སྒོམ་པ་རྒྱལ་སྲས་ལག་ལེན་ཡིན། །

གཉེན་གྱི་ཕྱོགས་ལ་འདོད་ཆགས་ཆུ་ལྟར་གཡོ། །
དགྲ་ཡི་ཕྱོགས་ལ་ཞེ་སྡང་མེ་ལྟར་འབར། །
བླང་དོར་བརྗེད་པའི་གཏི་མུག་མུན་ནག་ཅན། །
ཕ་ཡུལ་སྤོང་བ་རྒྱལ་སྲས་ལག་ལེན་ཡིན། །

ཡུལ་ངན་སྡུངས་པས་ཉེན་མོངས་རིམ་གྱིས་འགྲིབ། །
རྣམ་གཡེང་མེད་པས་དགེ་སྦྱོར་རང་གིས་འཕེལ། །
རིག་པ་དྭངས་པས་ཚོས་ལ་ངེས་ཤེས་སྐྱེ། །
དབེན་པ་བསྟེན་པ་རྒྱལ་སྲས་ལག་ལེན་ཡིན། ། ༣

ཡུན་རིང་འགྲོགས་པའི་མཛའ་བཤེས་སོ་སོར་འབྲལ། །
འབད་པས་བསྒྲུབས་པའི་ནོར་རྫས་ཤུལ་དུ་ལུས། །
ལུས་ཀྱི་མགྲོན་ཁང་རྣམ་ཤེས་མགྲོན་པོས་བོར། །
ཚེ་འདི་བློས་བཏང་རྒྱལ་སྲས་ལག་ལེན་ཡིན། ། ༤

གང་དང་འགྲོགས་ན་དུག་གསུམ་འཕེལ་འགྱུར་ཞིང་། །
ཐོས་བསམ་བསྒོམ་པའི་བྱ་བ་ཉམས་འགྱུར་ལ། །
བྱམས་དང་སྙིང་རྗེ་མེད་པར་བསྒྱུར་བྱེད་པའི། །
གྲོགས་ངན་སྤོང་བ་རྒྱལ་སྲས་ལག་ལེན་ཡིན། ། ༥

གང་ཞིག་བསྟེན་ན་ཉེས་པ་ཟད་འགྱུར་ཞིང་། །
ཡོན་ཏན་ཡར་ངོའི་ཟླ་ལྟར་འཕེལ་འགྱུར་བའི། །
བཤེས་གཉེན་དམ་པ་རང་གི་ལུས་བས་ཀྱང་། །
གཅེས་པར་འཛིན་པ་རྒྱལ་སྲས་ལག་ལེན་ཡིན། ། ༦

རང་ཡང་འཁོར་བའི་བཙོན་རར་བཅིངས་པ་ཡི། །
འཇིག་རྟེན་ལྷ་ཡིས་སུ་ཞིག་བསྐྱབ་པར་ནུས། །
དེ་ཕྱིར་གང་ལ་སྐྱབས་ན་མི་བསླུ་བའི། །
དཀོན་མཆོག་སྐྱབས་འགྲོ་རྒྱལ་སྲས་ལག་ལེན་ཡིན། ། ༧

ཤིན་ཏུ་བརྟེད་དགའི་ངན་སོང་སྒྲུག་བསྒྱལ་རྣམས། །
སྤྱིག་པའི་ལས་ཀྱི་འབྲས་བུར་ཐུབ་པས་གསུངས། །
དེ་ཕྱིར་སྡིག་ལ་བབ་ཀྱང་སྤྱིག་པའི་ལས། །
ནམ་ཡང་མི་བྱེད་རྒྱལ་སྲས་ལག་ལེན་ཡིན། །༥

སྲིད་གསུམ་བདེ་བ་རྩ་རྩེའི་ཟིལ་པ་བཞིན། །
ཡུད་ཚམ་ཞིག་གིས་འཇིག་པའི་ཆོས་ཅན་ཡིན། །
ནམ་ཡང་མི་འགྱུར་ཐར་པའི་གོ་འཕང་མཆོག །
དོན་དུ་གཉེར་བ་རྒྱལ་སྲས་ལག་ལེན་ཡིན། །༩

ཐོག་མེད་དུས་ནས་བདག་ལ་བརྩེ་བ་ཅན། །
མ་རྣམས་སྲྒྱུག་ན་རང་བདེས་ཅི་ཞིག་བྱ། །
དེ་ཕྱིར་མཐའ་ཡས་སེམས་ཅན་བསྒྲལ་བུའི་ཕྱིར། །
བྱང་རྒྱུབ་སེམས་བསྐྱེད་རྒྱལ་སྲས་ལག་ལེན་ཡིན། །༡༠

སྡུག་བསྒྱལ་མ་ལུས་བདག་བདེ་འདོད་ལས་བྱུང་། །
རྫོགས་པའི་སངས་རྒྱས་གཞན་ཕན་སེམས་ལས་འཁྲུངས། །
དེ་ཕྱིར་བདག་བདེ་གཞན་གྱི་སྡུག་བསྒྱལ་དག །
ཡང་དག་བརྗེ་བ་རྒྱལ་སྲས་ལག་ལེན་ཡིན། །༡༡

སུ་དག་འདོད་ཆེན་དབང་གིས་བདག་གི་ནོར། །
ཐམས་ཅད་འཕྲོག་གམ་འཕྲོག་ཏུ་འཇུག་ན་ཡང་། །
ལུས་དང་ལོངས་སྤྱོད་དུས་གསུམ་དགེ་བ་རྣམས། །
དེ་ལ་བསྔོ་བ་རྒྱལ་སྲས་ལག་ལེན་ཡིན། །༡༢

བདག་ལ་ཉེས་པ་ཅུང་ཟད་མེད་བཞིན་དུ། །
གང་དག་བདག་གིས་མགོ་བོ་གཡོགས་བྱེད་ནའང༌། །
སྙིང་རྗེའི་དབང་གིས་དེ་ཡི་སྡིག་པ་རྣམས། །
བདག་ལ་ལེན་པ་རྒྱལ་སྲས་ལག་ལེན་ཡིན། །༡༣

འགའ་ཞིག་བདག་ལ་མི་སྙན་སྣ་ཚོགས་པ། །
སྟོང་གསུམ་ཁྱབ་པར་སྒྲོག་པར་བྱེད་ན་ཡང༌། །
བྱམས་པའི་སེམས་ཀྱིས་སླར་ཡང་དེ་ཉིད་ཀྱི། །
ཡོན་ཏན་བརྗོད་པ་རྒྱལ་སྲས་ལག་ལེན་ཡིན། །༡༤

འགྲོ་མང་འདུས་པའི་དབུས་སུ་འགའ་ཞིག་གིས། །
མཚང་ནས་བྲུས་ཤིང་ཚིག་ངན་སྨྲ་ན་ཡང༌། །
དེ་ལ་དགེ་བའི་བཤེས་ཀྱི་འདུ་ཤེས་ཀྱིས། །
གུས་པར་འདུད་པ་རྒྱལ་སྲས་ལག་ལེན་ཡིན། །༡༥

བདག་གི་བུ་བཞིན་གཅེས་པར་བསྐྱངས་པའི་མིས། །
བདག་ལ་དགྲ་བཞིན་བལྟ་བར་བྱེད་ན་ཡང༌། །
ནད་ཀྱི་བཏབ་པའི་བུ་ལ་མ་བཞིན་དུ། །
ལྷག་པར་བརྩེ་བ་རྒྱལ་སྲས་ལག་ལེན་ཡིན། །༡༦

རང་དང་མཉམ་པའམ་དམན་པའི་སྐྱེ་བོ་ཡིས། །
ང་རྒྱལ་དབང་གིས་བརྙས་ཐབས་བྱེད་ན་ཡང༌། །
བླ་མ་བཞིན་དུ་གུས་པས་བདག་ཉིད་ཀྱི། །
སྤྱི་བོར་ལེན་པ་རྒྱལ་སྲས་ལག་ལེན་ཡིན། །༡༧

འཚོ་བས་ཕོངས་ཤིང་ཧྲག་ཏུ་མི་ཡིས་བརྙས། །

ཆབས་ཆེན་ནད་དང་གདོན་གྱིས་བཏབ་གྱུར་སྐྱར། །

འགྲོ་ཀུན་སྡིག་སྡུག་བདག་ལ་ལེན་བྱེད་ཅིང་། །

ཞུམ་པ་མེད་པ་རྐྱལ་སྲས་ལག་ལེན་ཡིན། ། ༡༢

སྣན་པར་གྲགས་ཤིང་འགྲོ་མང་སྤྱི་བོས་བཏུད། །

རྣམ་ཐོས་བུ་ཡི་ནོར་འདྲ་ཐོབ་གྱུར་ཀྱང་། །

སྲིད་པའི་དཔལ་འབྱོར་སྙིང་པོ་མེད་གཟིགས་ནས། །

ཁེངས་པ་མེད་པ་རྐྱལ་སྲས་ལག་ལེན་ཡིན། ། ༡༩

རང་གི་ཞེ་སྡང་དགྲ་བོ་མ་ཐུལ་ན། །

ཕྱི་རོལ་དགྲ་བོ་བཏུལ་ཞིང་འཕེལ་བར་འགྱུར། །

དེ་ཕྱིར་བྱམས་དང་སྙིང་རྗེའི་དམག་དཔུང་གིས། །

རང་རྒྱུད་འདུལ་བ་རྐྱལ་སྲས་ལག་ལེན་ཡིན། ། ༣༠

འདོད་པའི་ཡོན་ཏན་ལན་ཚྭའི་ཆུ་དང་འདྲ། །

ཇི་ཙམ་སྤྱད་ཀྱང་སྲེད་པ་འཕེལ་འགྱུར་བས། །

གང་ལ་ཞེན་ཆགས་སྐྱེ་བའི་དངོས་པོ་རྣམས། །

འཕྲལ་དུ་སྤོང་བ་རྐྱལ་སྲས་ལག་ལེན་ཡིན། ། ༣༡

ཇི་ལྟར་སྣང་བ་འདི་དག་རང་གི་སེམས། །

སེམས་ཉིད་གདོད་ནས་སྤྲོས་པའི་མཐའ་དང་བྲལ། །

དེ་ཉིད་ཤེས་ནས་གཟུང་འཛིན་མཚན་མ་རྣམས། །

ཡིད་ལ་མི་བྱེད་རྐྱལ་སྲས་ལག་ལེན་ཡིན། ། ༣༢

ཡིད་དུ་འོང་བའི་ཡུལ་དང་འཕྲད་པ་ན། །
དཔྱར་གྱི་དུས་ཀྱི་འཛའ་ཚོན་ཏེ་བཞིན་དུ། །
མཛེས་པར་སྣང་ཡང་བདེན་པར་མི་ལྟ་ཞིང་། །
ཞེན་ཆགས་སྤོང་བ་རྒྱལ་སྲས་ལག་ལེན་ཡིན། ། ༣༣

སྡུག་བསྔལ་སྣ་ཚོགས་རྨི་ལམ་བུ་ཤི་ལྟར། །
འཁྲུལ་སྣང་བདེན་པར་བཟུང་བས་ཨ་ཐང་ཆད། །
དེ་ཕྱིར་མི་མཐུན་རྐྱེན་དང་འཕྲད་པའི་ཚེ། །
འཁྲུལ་པར་ལྟ་བ་རྒྱལ་སྲས་ལག་ལེན་ཡིན། ། ༣༤

བྱང་ཆུབ་འདོད་པས་ལུས་ཀྱང་བཏང་དགོས་ན། །
ཕྱི་རོལ་དངོས་པོ་རྣམས་ལ་སྨོས་ཅི་དགོས། །
དེ་ཕྱིར་ལན་དང་རྣམ་སྨིན་མི་རེ་བའི། །
སྦྱིན་པ་གཏོང་བ་རྒྱལ་སྲས་ལག་ལེན་ཡིན། ། ༣༥

ཚུལ་ཁྲིམས་མེད་པར་རང་དོན་མི་འགྲུབ་ན། །
གཞན་དོན་སྒྲུབ་པར་འདོད་པ་གད་མོའི་གནས། །
དེ་ཕྱིར་སྲིད་པའི་འདུན་པ་མེད་པ་ཡི། །
ཚུལ་ཁྲིམས་བསྲུང་བ་རྒྱལ་སྲས་ལག་ལེན་ཡིན། ། ༣༦

དགེ་བའི་ལོངས་སྤྱོད་འདོད་པའི་རྒྱལ་སྲས་ལ། །
གནོད་བྱེད་ཐམས་ཅད་རིན་ཆེན་གཏེར་དང་མཚུངས། །
དེ་ཕྱིར་ཀུན་ལ་ཞེ་འགྲས་མེད་པ་ཡི། །
བཟོད་པ་སྐྱོམ་པ་རྒྱལ་སྲས་ལག་ལེན་ཡིན། ། ༣༧

རང་དོན་འབའ་ཞིག་བསྒྲུབ་པའི་ཉན་རང་ཡང་། །

མགོ་ལ་མེ་ཤོར་བསྙོག་ལྟར་བཙོན་མ་ཐོང་ན། །

འགྲོ་ཀུན་དོན་དུ་ཡོན་ཏན་འབྱུང་གནས་ཀྱི། །

འཚོན་འགྱུས་ཚེམ་པ་རྒྱལ་སྲས་ལག་ལེན་ཡིན། ། ༣༥

ཞི་གནས་རབ་ཏུ་ལྡན་པའི་ལྷག་མཐོང་གིས། །

ཉོན་མོངས་རྣམ་པར་འཇོམས་པར་ཤེས་བྱས་ནས། །

གཟུགས་མེད་བཞི་ལས་ཡང་དག་འདས་པ་ཡི། །

བསམ་གཏན་སྐྱོམ་པ་རྒྱལ་སྲས་ལག་ལེན་ཡིན། ། ༣༩

ཤེས་རབ་མེད་ན་ཕ་རོལ་ཕྱིན་ལྔ་ཡིས། །

རྫོགས་པའི་བྱང་ཆུབ་ཐོབ་པར་མི་ནུས་པས། །

ཐབས་དང་ལྡན་ཞིང་འཁོར་གསུམ་མི་རྟོག་པའི། །

ཤེས་རབ་སྐྱོམ་པ་རྒྱལ་སྲས་ལག་ལེན་ཡིན། ། ༣༠

རང་གི་འཁྲུལ་པ་རང་གིས་མ་བརྟགས་ན། །

ཆོས་པའི་གཟུགས་ཀྱིས་ཆོས་མིན་བྱེད་སྲིད་པས། །

དེ་ཕྱིར་རྒྱུན་དུ་རང་གི་འཁྲུལ་པ་ལ། །

བཏགས་ནས་སྤོང་བ་རྒྱལ་སྲས་ལག་ལེན་ཡིན། ། ༣༡

ཉོན་མོངས་དབང་གིས་རྒྱལ་སྲས་གཞན་དག་གི། །

ཉེས་པ་བྱུང་ན་བདག་ཉིད་འཛམས་འགྱུར་བས། །

ཐེག་པ་ཆེ་ལ་ཞུགས་པའི་གང་ཟག་གི། །

ཉེས་པ་མི་སྨྲ་རྒྱལ་སྲས་ལག་ལེན་ཡིན། ། ༣༢

རྙེད་བཀུར་དབང་གིས་ཕན་ཚུན་ཆོད་འགྱུར་ཞིང་། །
ཕོས་བསམ་སྐོམ་པའི་བུ་བ་ཉམས་འགྱུར་བས། །
མཛའ་བཤེས་ཁྱིམ་དང་སྙིན་བདག་ཁྱིམ་རྣམས་ལ། །
ཆགས་པ་སྤོང་བ་རྒྱལ་སྲས་ལག་ལེན་ཡིན། ། ༣༣

རྩུབ་མོའི་ཚིག་གིས་གཞན་སེམས་འཁྲུག་འགྱུར་ཞིང་། །
རྒྱལ་བའི་སྲས་ཀྱི་སྤྱོད་ཚུལ་ཉམས་འགྱུར་བས། །
དེ་ཕྱིར་གཞན་གྱི་ཡིད་དུ་མི་འོང་བའི། །
ཚིག་རྩུབ་སྤོང་བ་རྒྱལ་སྲས་ལག་ལེན་ཡིན། ། ༣༤

ཉོན་མོངས་གོམས་ན་གཉེན་པོས་བཟློག་དཀའ་བས། །
དྲན་ཤེས་སྐྱེས་བུས་གཉེན་པོའི་མཚོན་བཟུང་ནས། །
ཆགས་སོགས་ཉོན་མོངས་དང་པོ་སྐྱེས་མ་ཐག །
འབུར་འཛོམས་བྱེད་པ་རྒྱལ་སྲས་ལག་ལེན་ཡིན། ། ༣༥

མདོར་ན་གང་དུ་སྤྱོད་ལམ་ཅི་བྱེད་ཀྱང་། །
རང་གི་སེམས་ཀྱི་གནས་སྐབས་ཅི་འདུ་ཞེས། །
རྒྱུན་དུ་དྲན་དང་ཤེས་བཞིན་ལྡན་པ་ཡིས། །
གཞན་དོན་སྒྲུབ་པ་རྒྱལ་སྲས་ལག་ལེན་ཡིན། ། ༣༦

དེ་ལྟར་བཙོན་པས་བསྒྲུབ་པའི་དགེ་བ་རྣམས། །
མཐའ་ཡས་འགྲོ་བའི་སྡུག་བསྔལ་བསལ་བུའི་ཕྱིར། །
འཁོར་གསུམ་རྣམ་པར་དག་པའི་ཤེས་རབ་ཀྱིས། །
བྱང་རྒྱུབ་བསྔོ་བ་རྒྱལ་སྲས་ལག་ལེན་ཡིན། ། ༣༧

མདོ་རྒྱུད་བསྟན་བཅོས་རྣམས་ལས་གསུངས་པའི་དོན། །

དམ་པ་རྣམས་ཀྱི་གསུང་གི་རྗེས་འབྲང་ནས། །

རྒྱལ་སྲས་རྣམས་ཀྱི་ལག་ལེན་སྙམ་བུ་བདུན། །

རྒྱལ་སྲས་ལམ་ལ་སློབ་འདོད་དོན་དུ་བཀོད། །

བློ་གྲོས་དམན་ཞིང་སྦྱང་པ་ཆུང་བའི་ཕྱིར། །

མཁས་པ་དགྱེས་པའི་སྡེབ་སྦྱོར་མ་མཆིས་ཀྱང་། །

མདོ་དང་དམ་པའི་གསུང་ལ་བརྟེན་པའི་ཕྱིར། །

རྒྱལ་སྲས་ལག་ལེན་འཁྲུལ་མེད་ལགས་པར་བསམ། །

འོན་ཀྱང་རྒྱལ་སྲས་སྤྱོད་པ་རླབས་ཆེན་རྣམས། །

བློ་དམན་བདག་འདྲས་གཏིང་དཔག་དཀའ་བའི་ཕྱིར། །

འགལ་དང་མ་འབྲེལ་ལ་སོགས་ཉེས་པའི་ཚོགས། །

དམ་པ་རྣམས་ཀྱིས་བཟོད་པར་མཛད་དུ་གསོལ། །

དེ་ལས་བྱུང་བའི་དགེ་བས་འགྲོ་བ་ཀུན། །

དོན་དམ་ཀུན་རྫོབ་བྱང་རྒྱབ་སེམས་མཆོག་གིས། །

སྲིད་དང་ཞི་བའི་མཐའ་ལ་མི་གནས་པའི། །

སྤྱན་རས་གཟིགས་མགོན་དེ་དང་མཚུངས་པར་ཤོག །

ཅེས་པ་འདི་རང་གཞན་ལ་ཕན་པའི་དོན་དུ་ལྷུང་དང་རིགས་པ་སྨྲ་བའི་བཙུན་པ་ཐོགས་མེད་ཀྱིས་དངུལ་རྒྱལི་རིན་ཆེན་ཕུག་ཏུ་སྦྱར་བའོ།། །།

Acknowledgments

These talks could not have happened without the dedication and hard work of the nuns at Tilokpur Nunnery in India. They provided the perfect environment for the teachings to unfold. Ringu Tulku Rinpoche gave the oral translations for the talks, which were augmented with commentary by the Gyalwang Karmapa in the spring of 2008 and translated by Michele Martin. We are grateful to Sally Clay for her transcribing and initial editing of the Tilokpur talks. Appreciation goes to Lama Tashi Gawa for inputting the Tibetan text and to him and Chojor Radha for their kind advice on the translation. Daia Gerson provided her ever-excellent editing and Tracy Davis made great suggestions. Peter van Deurzen, Maureen McNicholas, and Florence Wetzel of KTD Publications kindly provided the context for the book to come to life. Naomi Schmidt of *Densal* has overseen the whole project, from asking the Gyalwang Karmapa for permission to publish up to formatting and designing the book. Our thanks extend around the globe to all those who have so generously contributed to this publication.

Karma Triyana Dharmachakra

Seat of His Holiness the Gyalwang Karmapa in North America

K arma Triyana Dharmachakra (KTD) is the North American seat of His Holiness the Gyalwang Karmapa, and under the spiritual guidance and protection of His Holiness Ogyen Trinley Dorje, the Seventeenth Gyalwang Karmapa, is devoted to the authentic representation of the Kagyu lineage of Tibetan Buddhism.

For information regarding KTD, including our current schedule, or for information regarding our affiliate centers, Karma Thegsum Chöling (KTCs), located both in the United States and internationally, contact us using the information below.

Karma Triyana Dharmachakra
335 Meads Mountain Road
Woodstock, NY 12498 USA
www.kagyu.org

Volume 19   Number 2

DENSAL
semiannual publication

D ensal is a bi-annual publicaton, featuring teaching, mostly given at Karma Triyana Dharmachakra, book excerpts from KTD publications, and relevant news from KTD. His Holiness the 16th Karmapa gave the name *Densal* to the KTD newsletter. It means "the clear truth." "He said, "It has a very strong meaning behind it. It is the work of Karma Triyana, through the Dharma, to bring truth to people with the greatest clarity possible."

This issue of *Densal* (Volume 19, Number 2) will not be available for purchase as a "back issue"; however the book will be available for purchase at Namse Bangdzo Bookstore.

Densal
Karma Triyana Dharmachakra
335 Meads Mountain Road
Woodstock, NY 12498
www.densal.org

KTD Publications

Gathering the garlands of the gurus' precious teachings

KTD Publications, a part of Karma Triyana Dharmachakra, is a not-for-profit publisher established with the purpose of facilitating the projects and activities manifesting from His Holiness Karmapa's inspiration and blessings. We are dedicated to gathering the garlands of precious teachings and producing fine-quality books.

KTD Publications
Karma Triyana Dharmachakra
335 Meads Mountain Road
Woodstock, NY 12498 USA
www.KTDPublications.org

Karma Drubgyu Thargay Ling

Mahayana Buddhist Nunnery, Tilokpur, India

Karma Drubgyu Thargay Ling in Tilokpur, India, is a practice center for nuns of the Kagyu Lineage of Tibetan Buddhism. It is about twenty miles southwest of Dharamsala. For many devoted women, the Buddhist Nunnery has provided the rare opportunity to be educated in and to practice the teachings of the Buddha.

KDTL receives economic support mainly from foreign sponsors and the Tibetan Nun's Project. This is generally in the form of sponsorship which pays only for the nuns basic living costs. The nuns also receive donations from individuals who request prayers and puja ceremonies. Now the nunnery needs to be improved and expanded so they will be able to accept nuns arriving from Tibet.

If you would like to assist towards the building and/or sponsor funds for the Tilokpur nuns you may donate to:

Karma Drubgyu Thargay Ling
Mahayana Buddhist Nunnery
P.O Tilokpur 176225
District Kangra, Himachal Pradesh
India
www.tilokpur.org